CROSSCURRENTS *Modern Critiques*

CROSSCURRENTS *Modern Critiques*
Harry T. Moore, *General Editor*

After the Genteel Tradition

AMERICAN WRITERS
1910 - 1930

EDITED BY *Malcolm Cowley*

WITH A PREFACE BY
Harry T. Moore

Carbondale

SOUTHERN ILLINOIS UNIVERSITY PRESS

To Van Wyck Brooks

—who will not agree with some of our ideas, but who
nevertheless helped us to reach them

FIRST PUBLISHED, MARCH 1964
SECOND PRINTING, JULY 1965

PREFACE

ALTHOUGH CROSSCURRENTS is not a reprint series, it will occasionally bring out up-to-date editions of notable books which have been for some time unobtainable. This applies to the present volume, the series' first reprint. After the Genteel Tradition, edited by Malcolm Cowley, first appeared in 1937. It more than deserves reissuing, for it is virtually the only full writer-by-writer study we have of the post-1910 rebel generation; and it is more than just that, for it is an exceptionally fine critical volume in its own right. Hence its reappearance here, with revisions.

Malcolm Cowley organized this book when he was literary editor of the New Republic. He held that position from 1929 to 1940, occasionally replaced, when on vacation, by the former literary editor, Edmund Wilson, or by Otis Ferguson (later to be one of America's Second World War casualties). In the thirties, in addition to its lively main section, liberal in the tradition of that time, the New Republic had the best-edited and most exciting literary section in the country. It dealt each week not with just a few specialized books but with the most important volumes then being published. Malcolm Cowley wrote the weekly lead review, a causerie that was always a delight to read: his comments on Hemingway, Dos Passos, Sinclair Lewis, and others were usually superior to those being made elsewhere. (I hope there is truth in the rumor that Henry Dan Piper is collecting these review-articles for publication.) Besides, the New Republic had a formidable battery of reviewers, some of whom are in the present volume, most of whose chapters were originally essays in that journal. The substance of other fine books first appeared also as New Republic essays, for example the principal chapters of Edmund Wilson's Axel's Castle and To the Finland Station. There was even another symposium volume, also made up of New Republic essays: Books That Changed Our Minds, edited by Malcolm Cowley and Bernard Smith; this included essays on Freud, Veblen, Lenin, Beard, Spengler, and others, by such critics as Mumford, Daiches, Lerner, and Radin.

Malcolm Cowley, in his revised introduction to the present edition of After the Genteel Tradition, says all that an introduction need say about the book, but I should like to note a point which he has made elsewhere: however social and political it may have been in 1937 (as illustrated by Robert Cantwell's judgment of Upton Sinclair), criticism was to an even greater extent moral. The chief moral standard was, as critics didn't really know then, Albert Schweitzer's: whether a work was life-enhancing or life-diminishing, a standard exemplified in Lionel Trilling's judgments of O'Neill and Cather, and in John Peale Bishop's evaluation of Hemingway's integrity. Also there was the question as to whether an author had faith, sympathy, love for the American people, and hope for their future: pessimism was condemned almost as strongly as it had been by the genteel critics twenty years earlier. Even the contributors to this volume whose slant is primarily historical—Malcolm Cowley and Peter Monro Jack—still applied these standards.

As Mr. Cowley has further pointed out, this socio-moral criticism was often weak on the connotative properties of language, though at least one liberal critic not represented here, Kenneth Burke, had taken that area as his specialty. For the most part, the criticism of the 1930s, with its interest in class conflicts and the historical processes and in authors representing social interests, with its emphasis on the meaning of moral decisions by the authors, with its correct notion that form and matter are interfused, and with its view that an author's withdrawal from society shows itself in the form of his work, like his confusion or pessimism or faith—with such preoccupations, this criticism took broader views than more recent criticism and addressed itself, though it didn't always reach it, to a wider audience.

Today, certainly, there will be a wide new audience for these significant evaluations, at once pioneering and durable, of the authors who broke with the genteel tradition. Mr. Cowley has not tampered with the original judgments of the contributors, but has put some of his introductory and concluding remarks into perspective and has augmented the literary calendar which is in itself an important contribution. After the Genteel Tradition provides an invigorating commentary upon our literary tradition and a link between American writing of yesterday and today. For anyone concerned with these subjects, it is an invaluable book, a welcome addition to the Crosscurrents series.

HARRY T. MOORE

Southern Illinois University
October 19, 1963

CONTENTS

x   CONTENTS

After the Genteel Tradition

AMERICAN WRITERS 1910–1930

FOREWORD:
THE REVOLT AGAINST GENTILITY

Malcolm Cowley

DECEMBER 10, 1930. At a meeting in Stockholm attended by the King of Sweden and the Swedish Academy, the Nobel Prize for Literature was presented to the author of *Main Street* and *Babbitt*. He was the first American to be measured and weighed and certified as an international giant of letters.

Judged from a purely literary point of view, he was neither the greatest nor the least of the Nobel prizemen. He was certainly not of the same stature as Kipling or Shaw or Thomas Mann (or, to add the names of American writers who died without getting the prize, as Mark Twain or Henry James). On the other hand, he was bigger by head and shoulders than many of the saga singers and little-problem playwrights whom the Swedish Academy had immortalized *pro tem*. When Sinclair Lewis won the prize, its literary value was neither enhanced nor diminished.

But I suppose that nobody is innocent enough to believe that the Nobel Prize is a purely literary event. Nobody imagines that the Swedish Academy confines its efforts to finding the very best living author, no matter what his nationality or the color of his opinions. Clearly there are diplomatic issues involved and questions of national honor. If a big country gets the prize one year, a small country is likely to get it the year after. If there is too much competition between Germany and France or

France and England, the difficulty can be avoided by naming a Dane or a Swede; some years it seems that almost anyone will do if he comes from the right country. It would be Italy's turn in 1934. That year we heard a pretty well substantiated rumor that the Italian ambassador in Stockholm had to engage in vigorous intrigues to keep the prize from going to Benedetto Croce, who was not a friend of Mussolini's. The successful candidate was Luigi Pirandello, who was politically inoffensive.

There was no whisper of backstairs maneuvering when Sinclair Lewis got the prize, and yet the choice in 1930 was unusually significant from the standpoint of world politics. During the sixteen years that began with the Great War, the United States had become not only a world power but industrially the greatest of the powers. American men of letters were supposed to have lagged behind American bankers and manufacturers, yet they could no longer be overlooked in favor of minor poets and short-story writers from Sicily, Lapland or wherever. When the Swedish Academy gave its medal and its forty thousand dollars to a man from Minnesota, it was saying in effect that American literature had ceased to be a minor province of British literature and must now be recognized in its own right.

The permanent secretary of the Swedish Academy, Erik Axel Karlfeldt, gave a speech of welcome in which he emphasized the national and international meaning of the prize (while revealing some ignorance of American history). "Yes," he said, "Sinclair Lewis is an American. He writes the new language—American—as one of the representatives of a hundred and twenty million souls. He asks us to consider that this nation is not yet finished or melted down; that it is still in the turbulent years of adolescence. The new great American literature has started with national self-criticism. It is a sign of health."

Two days later, when Lewis made his acceptance speech, he answered Dr. Karlfeldt as a lover and critic of America, as a representative of a hundred and twenty million souls. "The American Fear of Literature" was his subject. His address was front-page news in the American papers, and it remains a historical document of considerable meaning.

It seems that Dr. Henry Van Dyke had taken umbrage. Speaking as a member of the American Academy of Arts and Letters, this retired Princeton professor and former Presbyterian minister declaimed that the award of the Nobel Prize to a man who had scoffed so much at American institutions was an insult to our country. Lewis, after reporting the incident, suggested to his Swedish audience that Dr. Van Dyke might call out the Marines and have them landed in Stockholm to protect American literary rights. But he also had more serious comments to offer. Dr. Van Dyke, he said, was an almost official representative of the "genteel tradition" that for half a century had been the persistent enemy and slow poisoner of good writing in America:

> . . . most of us—not readers alone but even writers— are still afraid of any literature which is not a glorification of everything American, a glorification of our faults as well as our virtues. . . . We still most revere the writers for the popular magazines who in a hearty and edifying chorus chant that the America of a hundred and twenty million population is still as simple, as pastoral, as it was when it had but forty million . . . that, in fine, America has gone through the revolutionary change from rustic colony to world empire without having in the least altered the bucolic and Puritanic simplicity of Uncle Sam.

In the new American empire it was possible for a writer to make plenty of money: he could have his butler and his motor and his villa at Palm Beach, where he could mingle almost on terms of equality with the barons of banking. But still, if he took his profession seriously,

> . . . he is oppressed by something worse than poverty— by the feeling that what he creates does not matter, that he is expected by his readers to be only a decorator or a clown, or that he is good-naturedly accepted as a scoffer whose bark is probably worse than his bite and who certainly does not count in a land that produces eighty-story buildings, motors by the million and wheat by the billions

of bushels. And he has no institution, no group, to which he can turn for inspiration, whose criticism he can accept and whose praise will be precious to him.

Lewis began to call the roll of the groups or institutions that ought to be friendly to creative writing. The American Academy? It contains so very few of the first-rate writers that "it does not represent literary America of today—it represents only Henry Wadsworth Longfellow." The American universities? Four of them have shown some real interest in contemporary creative literature: "Rollins College in Florida, Middlebury College in Vermont, the University of Michigan, and the University of Chicago." But most of the others have exemplified "the divorce in America of intellectual life from all authentic standards of importance and reality. . . . To a true-blue professor of American literature in an American university, literature is not something that a plain human being, living today, painfully sits down to produce. No, it is something dead; it is something magically produced by superhuman beings who must, if they are to be regarded as artists at all, have died at least one hundred years before the diabolical invention of the typewriter." And what about our literary criticism? "Most of it," Lewis said, "has been a chill and insignificant activity pursued by jealous spinsters, ex-baseball reporters, and acid professors." There have been no valid standards because there has been nobody capable of setting them up. Worse still, there have been the false and life-denying standards of critics like William Dean Howells and Henry Van Dyke, who were "effusively seeking to guide America into becoming a pale edition of an English cathedral town."

Fortunately, Lewis continued, the younger generation has untied itself from their stepmotherly apron strings. A whole new literature has come of age, a literature that tries to express the sweep and strength and beauty-in-ugliness of the American empire as it is today. There are a dozen American writers worthy of receiving the Nobel Prize. But no matter which of them had been chosen, there would have been the same outcry from the academicians and from the New Humanists drily embattled in their college libraries.

ii

    In the most significant part of his speech, Lewis enumerated the great men and great achievements of the 1920's. He imagined what the older and more genteel critics would have said to each possible choice of the Swedish Academy:

    Suppose you had taken Theodore Dreiser.

    Now to me, as to many other American writers, Dreiser more than any other man, marching alone, usually unappreciated, often hated, has cleared the trail from Victorian and Howellsian timidity and gentility in American fiction to honesty and boldness and passion of life. Without his pioneering, I doubt if any of us could, unless we liked to be sent to jail, express life and beauty and terror. . . .

    Yet had you given the prize to Mr. Dreiser, you would have heard groans from America; you would have heard . . . that his style is cumbersome, that his choice of words is insensitive, that his books are interminable. And certainly respectable scholars would complain that in Mr. Dreiser's world, men and women are often sinful and tragic and despairing, instead of being forever sunny and full of song and virtue, as befits authentic Americans.

    And had you chosen Mr. Eugene O'Neill, who has done nothing much in American drama save to transform it utterly, in ten or twelve years, from a false world of neat and competent trickery to a world of splendor and fear and greatness, you would have been reminded that he has done something far worse than scoffing—he has seen life as not to be neatly arranged in the study of a scholar but as a terrifying, magnificent and often quite horrible thing akin to the tornado, the earthquake, the devastating fire.

    And had you given Mr. James Branch Cabell the prize, you would have been told that he is too fantastically malicious. So would you have been told that Miss Willa Cather, for all the homely virtue of her novels concerning the peasants of Nebraska, has in her novel, "A Lost

Lady," been so untrue to America's patent and perpetual and possibly tedious virtuousness as to picture an abandoned woman who remains, nevertheless, uncannily charming even to the virtuous, in a story without any moral; that Mr. Henry Mencken is the worst of all scoffers; that Mr. Sherwood Anderson viciously errs in considering sex as important a force in life as fishing; that Mr. Upton Sinclair, being a Socialist, sins against the perfectness of American capitalistic mass production; that Mr. Joseph Hergesheimer is un-American in regarding graciousness of manner and beauty of surface as of some importance in the endurance of daily life; and that Mr. Ernest Hemingway is not only too young but, far worse, uses language which should be unknown to gentlemen; that he acknowledges drunkenness as one of man's eternal ways to happiness. . . .

Dreiser and O'Neill, James Branch Cabell, Willa Cather, H. L. Mencken, Sherwood Anderson, Upton Sinclair, Joseph Hergesheimer and Ernest Hemingway: this list of distinguished writers needs a few emendations. The speaker himself should most certainly be added to it. So too should Van Wyck Brooks, the first critic to express many of the ideas that Lewis was presenting to the Swedish Academy. So too should Frost and Robinson, as well as "the really original and vital poets, Edna St. Vincent Millay and Carl Sandburg, Robinson Jeffers and Vachel Lindsay and Edgar Lee Masters," mentioned in another passage of the same address. On the other hand, Hemingway might have been omitted here, since he belongs by age and spirit to another generation. But with a very few changes of this order, the list would be definitive. Sinclair Lewis, in his speech at Stockholm, had named the prominent figures of the era in American literature that was just then drawing to a close.

But he did more than merely catalogue the "great men and women in American literary life today." He also specified the reasons for their greatness (and in quoting what the academic critics would say against them he was praising them still more, by indirection). Thus, Dreiser had "cleared the way from Victorian and Howellsian timidity and gentility." O'Neill had seen life "as not to be neatly arranged in the study of a scholar." Willa Cather had been "so untrue to America's patent and perpetual and possibly tedious virtuousness as to picture an abandoned woman . . . in a story without any moral" (though the moral was so patently there that Lewis must have been trying not to find it). Mencken had offended the godly by scoffing at evangelism; Anderson had offended them by not scoffing at sex; and even Hemingway had fitted into the pattern of negation and defiance by using "language which should be unknown to a gentleman." It seemed to Lewis that all these authors were united into one crusading army by their revolt against the genteel tradition.

iii

But what was the nature of this tradition against which so many writers had rebelled?

In part it was an attempt to abolish the evils and vulgarities and sometimes the simple changes in American society by never talking about them. It had some connection with the English movement or manner that was later known as Victorianism, but it was even more stringent in its prohibitions, possibly because the evils in a younger society were harder not to mention. It also had a connection with the Civil War. The war has been so idealized by genteel novelists and historians that we find it hard to recognize a simple fact: it was a war like any other, with its normal share of pillage, drunkenness, filth, profiteering and disorder. Moreover, the wartime atmosphere was prolonged through the Reconstruction years, which were the years of lawlessness in the South and financial corruption in the North; the years when millions of immigrants were crowding into the slums; the gaudy and vicious years when bribe-taking congressmen had to push their way through a crowd of prostitutes as they climbed the steps of the Capitol.

It is no wonder that there was a moral reaction, which gained strength after the panic of 1873. The pity is that much or most of the reaction was not directed toward the real evils of American life at the time. Instead the chief effort of many reformers was focused on the American middle-class home and its presiding spirit, the pure young girl. The reformers tried to keep them both unsullied by ignoring or denying the brutalities of business life. Every cultural object that entered the home was supposed to express the highest ideals and aspirations. Every book or magazine intended to appear on the center table in the parlor was kept as innocent as milk. American women of all ages, especially the unmarried ones, had suddenly become more than earthly creatures; they were presented as milk-white angels of art and compassion and culture. "It is the 'young girl' and the family center table," Frank Norris complained in the 1890's, "that determine the standard of the American short story."

Scribner's, Harper's and the Century were the principal voices of the genteel era. Their standard of fiction was fairly high in a literary sense, and I suspect that better magazines for a wide audience have never been published in this country; but in matters of decorum the standard was that of a rather strict girls' boarding school. Richard Watson Gilder, who edited the Century from 1881 to 1909, once refused to print a war story that he had already accepted. His change of mind was caused by a sentence he had missed on a first reading: "The bullet had left a blue mark over the brown nipple." Even William Dean Howells sometimes failed to meet his schoolmistressly standards. When the Century was serializing The Rise of Silas Lapham, Gilder had the presses stopped in order to delete a reference to dynamite in labor disputes. Roger Burlingame, the distinguished editor of Scribner's, rejected an early novel by Hamlin Garland on the comprehensive ground that it contained "slang, profanity, vulgarity, agnosticism, and radicalism." Harper's, edited for fifty years by Henry Mills Alden, was a little more worldly than its two great rivals; it went so far as to accept Hardy's Jude the Obscure. But before printing the novel in monthly instalments, it imposed two conditions on the author: the children of Jude and Sue, born out of wedlock, had to be presented as adopted orphans, and the title had to be changed to *Hearts Insurgent*.

No such conditions had been imposed in England. The greater stringency or prissiness of American editors might be explained by a change in the Victorian proprieties after they crossed the Atlantic. In Boston and New York they acquired some provincial or native characteristics, and notably they became intermingled with a late and debased form of New England puritanism. Of course the original Puritans were not in the least genteel. Believing in the real existence of evil, they denounced it in language that was not intended for the young girl or the family center table. But their doctrines had been transformed by the years, and the puritanism of their descendants was hardly more than a set of rules and a tendency to divide practical life from the life of the mind, just as Sunday was divided from the days of the week. In *America's Coming-of-Age* Van Wyck Brooks discusses the tendency with much acuteness. Practical life, he says, had become a hard, dirty scramble in which the only justifiable aim was to get ahead, be successful, make money, but meanwhile the life of the mind was supposed to be kept as spotless and fragrant with lavender as a white Sunday dress. The two sides of this later puritanism might be those of a single man: for example, Andrew Carnegie, who made a fortune by manufacturing armor plate and then spent it in promoting peace by impractical methods and in building libraries where the men in his rolling mills, who worked twelve hours a day and seven days a week, would never have time to read masterworks. Culture was something reserved and refined for the Sunday people: women, ministers, university professors and the readers of genteel magazines.

But the Victorian spirit in America was also intermingled with the defiant optimism that grew out of pioneering and land speculation. There were always better farms to the westward. Prices would always go up, and the mortgage would be paid at the last moment, while the sheriff was pounding at the door. . . . With this background of belief, many American books had the same innocently hopeful atmosphere as American real-estate developments; they were like cement sidewalks laid down in the wilderness with the absolute certainty that, some day, there would be a skyscraper on this corner lot now covered with sagebrush. To fail or simply to be discouraged in the midst of so many opportunities was not only a sign of weakness; it was a sin like adultery, and it could scarcely be mentioned in novels written for decent people.

Those two characteristics of the genteel tradition in America—I mean its absolute divorce from daily life (or its "ideality," in the language of genteel critics) and its high optimism—were part of what Marxists would call its ideological superstructure. It also possessed, however, a pretty firm base in American society. It could depend on popular support because, in many social conflicts of the time, the genteel writers all represented the side that was older and firmly entrenched.

Thus, in the conflict between city ideals and country ideals, they all took the rural side. The United States in 1890 was already becoming urbanized and industrialized, and most of the genteel writers had followed the times by moving to New York or Boston; but the ideals they defended in their writing were those of an earlier day. "In a hearty and edifying chorus," as Lewis said, they chanted that this was still a nation of villagers devoted to plain living and high thinking.

In the conflict between the Eastern seaboard and the Middle West, most of the genteel writers represented the seaboard—and particularly New York and New England—no matter where they had been born. They found some room in their company for Southern writers, mostly local colorists, and later they admitted a whole school of Indiana novelists who yearned for the days when knighthood was in flower. They did not believe, however, that the Middle West of their own time was a proper subject for fiction. Hamlin Garland once complained that so far as the literary magazines were concerned, "Wisconsin, Minnesota and Iowa did not exist. Not a picture, not a single poem or story, not even a reference to those states could I discover in ten thousand pages of print."

In the conflict of racial strains, always fiercer in this country than historians like to admit, the genteel writers all represented the older immigration. They were English by descent, except for a few whose forebears were Scottish or Knickerbocker or Huguenot, and they looked down in a kindly way on the Irish and the Germans. England for them was "our old home," to be regarded with a mixture of emulative jealousy and pride of kinship. Their literary models were English, with the result that much of their writing seemed less national than colonial.

In matters of religion they were almost all Protestant by training, and many of them were church-going Episcopalians or Presbyterians all their lives. Those who lost their faith became Protestant agnostics, a very different breed from Catholic or from Jewish agnostics. They could not imagine a time when the United States might be anything else than a Protestant nation.

In politics they were civil-service reformers, Mugwumps in 1884, Bull Moosers in 1912, and strongly pro-British in the Great War. But the conflict in which they played the longest part was the old one between the rich and the poor, or rather—since the truly poor had found no voice in American letters—between the old rich families and the lower middle class. They chose their side without much hesitation, as a rule, though Howells and Garland both had struggles of conscience. Many of the genteel writers were themselves poor devils living in furnished rooms, but the world presented in their stories was that of people who always dressed for dinner and never talked about money, being too well bred. Theodore Dreiser, who knew nothing of that world, wondered how he could possibly write for the leading magazines. He says at the end of *A Book about Myself*:

> In a kind of ferment or fever due to my necessities and desperation, I set to examining the current magazines and

the fiction and articles to be found therein: *Century, Scribner's, Harper's*. I was never more confounded than by the discrepancy existing between my own observations and those displayed here, the beauty and peace and charm to be found in everything, the almost complete absence of any reference to the coarse and the vulgar. . . .

Maybe such things were not the true province of fiction anyhow. I read and read, but all I could gather was that I had no such tales to tell, and, however much I tried, I could not think of any. The kind of thing I was witnessing no one would want as fiction. These writers seemed far above the world of which I was a part. Indeed I began to picture them as creatures of the greatest luxury and culture, gentlemen and ladies all, comfortably housed, masters of servants, possessing estates, or at least bachelor quarters, having horses and carriages, and received here, there and everywhere with nods of recognition and smiles of approval.

That was a lonely young man's picture of the genteel writers, but it was not wholly false. A few of them were truly men of substance, the intimate friends of millionaires, and they were models of conduct for the others. Even the poor devils in furnished rooms might hope for invitations to one of the great dinners at which Andrew Carnegie entertained the literary world. And the genteel tradition not only had wealthy patrons; it also had powerful institutions of its own. Besides the three great magazines and their respectable poor relations, the *Atlantic* and the *North American Review*, there were also the established publishing houses, most of which were glad to instruct their authors in the rules for meeting the genteel taste, besides furnishing them with subjects and, on occasion, with readymade plots. There were the great Eastern universities, given over to the promotion of culture, football and ideality. I remember a Leyendecker lithograph of a blondely handsome football team running out on the field in clean blue jerseys. Under it was an inscription that revealed the feeling of the time:

> Go, lose or conquer as ye can:
> Be each, pray God, the gentleman!

In New York there were many clubs that welcomed young writers who were also gentlemen, praise God: there were the Century, the Authors', the Players', the Lotos, the Aldine, the National Arts, some of them endowed by millionaires, and there were also the Bohemians in San Francisco and the Cliff Dwellers in Chicago, this last founded by Hamlin Garland, who described himself as "a great carpenter and joiner of clubs." In New York again there was the National Institute of Arts and Letters, with its Department of Literature that was, until 1930, almost wholly confined to genteel writers. The American Academy, which Lewis attacked with such violence (and to which he would be proud of being elected in 1937), was the inner circle of the Institute.

All these institutions together provided an imposing display of literary power and status. A young author of talent, if he was sufficiently genteel, might appear in the *Century* or *Harper's*, might be offered a contract for a novel to be serialized in the same magazine before being published in hard covers, might lecture on the Chautauqua circuit, might be elected to one or more of the endowed clubs, then to the National Institute, and might look forward to having his works published in a collected edition, like those of Thomas Nelson Page and F. Hopkinson Smith—though he might become so entranced with club life and dinners at big houses that he had little time for written works. But if the young writer insisted on being pessimistic; if he portrayed women whose virtue was not laced in whalebone stays—or if he insisted on writing about "religion, love, politics, alcohol or fairies," as one great editor advised Edith Wharton not to do—then the doors of the institutions were closed to him. He might still achieve a career if he had some quite rare advantage, like Mrs. Wharton's wealth or Frank Norris's lion-cub friendliness and energy or Stephen Crane's genius, but there were a thousand chances of failure to one of success.

The wonder is that young writers had courage enough to rebel against all this entrenched power. We know that many lost heart and that some of the best—Crane,

Norris, Trumbull Stickney—died in their early thirties as if worn out by the struggle. But other young writers succeeded them and, in the course of time, they set themselves against every feature of the genteel tradition. Instead of being Puritans in the cant sense of the word, many of them were frankly sensual, given to praising sexual freedom and to justifying drunkenness "as one of man's eternal ways to happiness." Instead of being optimistic, they painted a world in which "men and women are often sinful and tragic and despairing." Instead of belonging to the North Atlantic seaboard, most of them boasted of having roots in the Middle West or the South. Instead of being inspired by English models, they either tried to create an American myth, in the American language, with saints and folk heroes like Abe Lincoln and Johnny Appleseed, or else they followed theories like socialism and Freudianism that had originated on the continent of Europe. But most of all, the new literary movement was a revolt of the lower middle classes against conventions that did not fit their personal lives and that prevented them from telling the truth about their world. On this last point Lewis was as eloquent as Dreiser:

> I had realized in reading Balzac and Dickens that it was possible to describe French and English common people as one actually saw them. But it had never occurred to me that one might without indecency write of the people of Sauk Centre, Minnesota, as one felt about them. Our fictional tradition, you see, was that all of us in Midwestern villages were altogether noble and happy; that not one of us would exchange the neighborly bliss of living on Main Street for the heathen gaudiness of New York or Paris or Stockholm. But in Mr. Garland's "Main-Traveled Roads" I discovered that Midwestern peasants were sometimes bewildered and hungry and vile—and heroic. And, given this vision, I was released; I could write of life as living life.

Hamlin Garland, after writing two good books, Lewis said, "had gone to Boston and become cultured and Howellsized"; but the somewhat younger writers whom

Lewis was praising had kept their vigor and honesty by resisting the genteel influences. They had in fact created a new literature that was as broad and native as the prairies. "As a chauvinistic American," Lewis said, "—only, mind you, as an American of 1930 and not of 1880—I can rejoice that they are my countrymen, and that I can speak of them with pride, even in the Europe of Thomas Mann, H. G. Wells, Galsworthy, Knut Hamsun. . . ." He did not believe that they had yet affected the public at home. "It is not today vastly more true than it was twenty years ago that . . . novelists like Dreiser and Willa Cather are authentically popular and influential in America." He thought that they still had to fight their war of liberation. But in this idea, so it seems to us today, he was at least ten years behind the times.

The war was already under way in 1890, but the decisive battles had been fought in the decade after 1910, when almost every new writer was a recruit to the army against gentility, and when older writers like Dreiser and Robinson were being rescued from neglect and praised as leaders. In those days Mabel Dodge's salon, the Provincetown Playhouse and, in Chicago, the Dill Pickle Club were the rallying grounds of the rebel forces. The *Masses* (1911), *Poetry* (1912), the *Smart Set* (of which the best year was 1913) and the *Little Review* (1914) were its propaganda organs.

In "A Literary Calendar: 1911–1930," at the end of this volume, I have tried to list the principal events in that war against the genteel tradition. For a time every honestly written book was a foray against the conservatives, and some were resounding victories—as notably *Jennie Gerhardt* (1911), America's *Coming-of-Age* and *Spoon River Anthology* (1915), *Chicago Poems* (1916), *The Education of Henry Adams* (1918), *Winesburg, Ohio* and *Our America* (1919). The battle over *Jurgen*, beginning that same year, ended as a major triumph over the censors. In 1920 came the success of *Beyond the Horizon*, the first play by one of the rebels to be produced on Broadway, and the vastly greater success of *Main Street*.

The novel was published by Harcourt, Brace and Howe, one of several new publishing houses that supported the new writers. The older houses—even Charles Scribner's Sons, which had been the most conservative—were beginning to take more chances. As for the genteel critics, by 1920 they were fighting rearguard actions to protect their line of retreat. When Lewis renewed the battle ten years later, he was vastly overestimating the strength of his surviving enemies, so that an element of farce was mingled with the drama of his Stockholm address. For the truth was that Dr. Henry Van Dyke had lost his influence except with elderly grade-school teachers and with low-church Episcopalian rectors in the suburbs. The truth was that the whole decade of the 1920's had been dominated by the nongenteel, non-Anglican, nonidealistic writers. And the Swedish Academy, by deciding to honor a member of the group, had raised it to the highest point it would ever reach, to a mild and general apotheosis.

iv

Lewis's address might have received still more attention in the press, but that month it had to compete for attention with events of a different sort. On December 11, 1930, the day after the ceremony in Stockholm, the Bank of United States closed its doors. It had fifty-nine branches, all in New York City, and four hundred thousand depositors, and its failure was the biggest so far in a series of bankruptcies that threatened the entire banking system. The country was entering the second year of the depression. The number of unemployed was not accurately known, but was rising from week to week; by December it must have been six or seven million. Nobody felt sure of his business or his farm or his pay envelope for Saturday after next. In the midst of the general uneasiness new political currents were swirling; the Democrats had won their first majority in Congress since 1916; the Communists were attracting their first disciples since 1920. There were new literary currents too; people were revising their attitudes toward reading and writing along with everything else. Many established writers of the 1920's were about to lose their public and lapse into silence, or into the *Saturday Evening Post,* or else to deny their past and set out in a variety of new directions.

"The years since then," I wrote in 1937 when this book first appeared, "have given us perspective enough to re-value the whole school that Sinclair Lewis was representing and glorifying at Stockholm. It would be easy to condemn these writers as a group, and the fact is that they have already been sentenced and mass-executed a dozen times. But they have clearly done too much to merit that quick treatment. They established—or, if we remember Concord, they reëstablished—the profession of letters in America. They made it possible for young Americans to write without a side-glance at London or Oxford, to speak in their own language about everyday matters, to be accurate, coarse, even bawdy, without too much fear of having their books suppressed—or stored in a publisher's cellar like *Sister Carrie*—because they were thought to contain an objectionable situation.

"But beyond all that," I continued, "what were these writers really saying? What were they trying to do, as individuals, and to what degree did they fulfill their aims? Which of them belonged merely to their own age of easy reputations, when the great American novel was being published every week, and which of them have strength enough to survive into a harsher era? These are questions that a dozen critics, most of them belonging to a some-what younger generation, are trying to answer in the chapters that follow."

There is no reason to change those words in 1964, but I have made some changes in my other contributions to the book, as, for example, in the earlier sections of this Fore-word, where the original text failed to explain that the genteel tradition was something more than a set of con-ventions. I have expanded the Literary Calendar, so as to make it a better means of suggesting the relation between events in the writer's world and those in the world at large, and I have rounded out the book by adding a chapter on Edwin Arlington Robinson written in 1948. I thought of including Frost as well, but his work stands somewhat apart from the movement we were trying to revalue. Robinson is more directly involved in the story. He issued no proclamations, but among our poets of stature he is the one who paid the highest price in his life for having rejected optimism and ideality.

I have made no change in the judgments expressed in 1937, though some are a little different from my judgments today, and I did not suggest to the eleven other critics that they should revise the chapters they each contributed. Some of their prophecies have been contradicted by events, as notably Hamilton Basso's final remark about Thomas Wolfe: "Learn 'em I think he will." Learn 'em he might have done, if he had lived longer, but he died a year after Basso's chapter was written. In passing judgment on Upton Sinclair's novels, Robert Cantwell mingles literature and politics in the fashion of the 1930's; he says that Sinclair "has been the outstanding literary representative of the Second International," as indeed he was for a long time, "in the same way that a writer of the type of André Malraux—intense, defiant, scornful— promises now to become the voice in fiction of the hard-pressed and violent life of the Third." Two or three years later Malraux would stop writing fiction even before he turned against the Communist International. I think it would be a mistake, however, for Cantwell or Basso to change these statements, which carry a date stamped into the words; let them stand for the record. Most of the book is as valid today as when it was written. In revising it for a new edition I tried to preserve its double value, first as a revaluation of twenty years in American literary history, a time of immense changes, and then as a historical document in itself, a record of what the younger critics were saying in 1937.

THEODORE DREISER

John Chamberlain

I WAS DRIVING EAST from Chicago, when I passed through Warsaw, Indiana, a sleepy town situated close to three small, lovely lakes. There was something familiar about the place, something that made me feel certain I had been there before. Then suddenly I remembered: I had read about Warsaw in Theodore Dreiser's autobiography of childhood, *Dawn*. Dreiser had lived there in his early teens; there in the local library he had read Shakespeare, Ouida, *Tom Jones*, Laura Jean Libby, General Lew Wallace's *Ben Hur*, Dickens, Carlyle and *Moll Flanders* in higgledy-piggledy confusion. There one of his sisters had conceived an illegitimate child; there his mother, a vague, sweet, struggling, ineffectual creature, had tried to keep the remnants of her family together on practically nothing. And there young Theo had skated and swum, had mooned about the beauty of the lakes and the Tippecanoe River, and had dreamed about high-born girls while having an experience with the baker's willing daughter.

It was easy to imagine the culture of Warsaw two or three generations ago; you could read it in the town's architecture, which was a little more solid than Rochester's to the south, or that of Coldwater, Michigan, to the north. Quite obviously the culture had been Puritan-commercial; that could be taken for granted. But—or so one fancied—the spirit of the place wasn't too pushing or too intolerant. The local church sociables were really sociable; it was, in short, the sort of town that would neither accept the Dreisers nor persecute them; nor would it try to bring these impoverished newcomers from southern Indiana into the Puritan-commercial orbit.

I had not read Dreiser in a long time and I had not been thinking of him. But the five minutes spent driving through Warsaw suddenly explained to me Dreiser's relation to the literature of his times and to the movement of ideas that killed the rule of the genteel tradition in America. This was not the result of an attempt at mystical penetration on my part; I was no Keyserling catching an idea from a cross-wind merely because the car had slowed down to fifteen miles an hour. What had happened was that the half-remembered facts of *Dawn* suddenly shuffled themselves into a significant pattern. Dreiser, it became obvious to me for the first time, had not consciously attacked the sway of the genteel tradition when he wrote *Sister Carrie*. That book was a yea-saying to what he had learned in Warsaw, not a nay-saying to the conventional New England schoolmarm. Indeed, his own school teachers had been both sympathetic and helpful.

Consider the facts in the case. The young Theodore had not been accepted by Puritan-commercial folk; therefore he was not loaded down in childhood with hampering theories of the correct way in which to live and act and write. The great moral paradox of the age—how to square the competitive parable of the talents with other teachings of the New Testament—did not trouble him, since he was not preached at by elders who were quick to urge young people to succeed, and to be good Christian men and women at the same time. Nor did he suffer because of exclusion: Warsaw did not hound him. He got through the impressionable years without undue infection from the missionary spirit of the American Tract Society and the novels of the period. Instead, he followed his instincts: for sentimentalism (Ouida, Laura Jean Libby), and for good, raw, healthily vulgar stuff (*Tom Jones, Moll Flanders*). The Ouida strain and the *Tom Jones* strain persist as dominants in all the Dreiser books. If young Theodore had anything to rebel against, anything to give him the mark of negativism, it was the Catholic Church, whose creed was interpreted with a dogmatic literalness by his narrow and repellent father. But the father, who did not come with his family to Warsaw, lacked the intelligence to apply the Catholic creed to books or to daily life; his dogmatism remained largely *in vacuo*. Hence Dreiser's opposition to his father never centered on anything concrete. It developed merely into an animus against philosophy in general and so served to confirm him in an empirical habit of mind.

The women of Dreiser's novels are generally of two types—the uncritical, naturally sweet sort who give in for reasons of sympathy rather than of passion, and the prim, fussy daughters of the genteel. The first type—Carrie Meeber, Jennie Gerhardt, Roberta Alden, even Aileen Butler, the contractor's daughter, of *The Financier* and *The Titan*—is compounded of Dreiser's memories of his mother and his sisters; the second type is obviously drawn from the model of his first wife, a Missouri girl who was his first contact with the genteel. But the girl from Missouri had nothing to do with the shape of *Sister Carrie* or *Jennie Gerhardt*; these books are positive acts, affirmations of life hungering for experience. Not until he wrote *The Genius* and, later on, *An American Tragedy* did Dreiser mix animus with his ink. The animus is probably the reason for his heavy insistence on the role of environment in accounting for the character of Clyde Griffiths. Simply because the conscious nay-sayer protests too much, it has been easy to attack the conception of the young Clyde as "inevitably" the product of his early environment. Other young men with evangelical backgrounds failed to kill their sweethearts in similar dilemmas. Theory, in Dreiser's later years, commenced to ride his feeling for personality; he did better work when he was concerned with projecting personality, leaving the moralizing for isolated passages that stand as blemishes without destroying the force of his creation.

It is the early Dreiser that interests me—the Dreiser

of *Carrie* and *Jennie*, of the Cowperwood stories, and of
the autobiographical narrative, *A Book About Myself*,
later republished as *Newspaper Days*. I read *A Book
About Myself* when I was just out of college, a young
innocent who had little idea of what made the wheels go
round in America. With its detailed account of wandering
through Chicago, St. Louis, Toledo, Pittsburgh and New
York in the nineties, *A Book About Myself* made the
complexity of the modern industrial scene understandable—one could see from Dreiser's weltering, wondering,
patient pages how it came into being. Dreiser's memories
of the Pittsburgh of the Homestead Strike were especially
galvanic; I had scarcely known, before reading *A Book
About Myself*, that such a thing as labor strife existed.
(We were then living in the New Era, and I had been too
young to take any particular notice of the troubles of
1918–21.) *A Book About Myself* was just the thing to
give a fledgeling newspaper reporter a sense of orienta-
tion. As for the novels—*Carrie, Jennie, The Titan, The
Financier*—they helped to confirm the impressions gained
from *A Book About Myself*. But they don't stand intensive
rereading; one recalls them too easily. They have no
stubborn subtleties of the sort that only yield themselves
up on the third trip; hence my main affection for
Dreiser is that he once helped me and did such a good job
of it that I need his help no longer. Along with Scott
Fitzgerald, Ring Lardner and others, he taught me to see
through the genteel tradition, to shake myself free of the
belated colonialism of the late nineteenth century in
New England. He taught me to discount as wish fulfilment the ideas of Stuart P. Sherman, who seemed to think
Carrie Meebers and Jennie Gerhardts and Frank Cow-
perwoods were impossible.

Not that Dreiser's anatomy of American life is final; no
live person's should be. Finality means the end of curiosity,
and Dreiser has always been curious. Even his late attempt
to square Marxism with his own notions of "equity" leaves
plenty of room for discovery, for rearranging his patterns
to account for new intrusions of fact. He is still the

empiricist. This habit of mind was what distinguished him, along with Stephen Crane, from all his important novelist contemporaries. And because of this habit of mind and a set of reflexes that had not been conditioned by the dominant ethos, the young Dreiser went forth, equipped as no other novelist of the late nineteenth century, to understand emerging industrial America. When he looked at a "captain of industry" or a "promoter," he was under no inner compulsion to square what he saw with an ethic picked up in Sunday-school years. Herein he broke with more tender-minded contemporary novelists who were also fascinated by the problem of industrial power—with Frank Norris, William Allen White and Robert Herrick, besides a host of lesser figures. The lesser figures were content to shut their eyes and glorify; they did the groundwork that resulted in the Coolidge cult of Service. To Norris, White and Herrick, more sensitive men, the industrialist was too patent a force to be ignored, yet they couldn't digest him without serious qualms of conscience.

The business man was justified by the parable of the talents, yes; but there was this matter of the plain words of the New Testament. What to do about the paradox? William Allen White solved it, in *A Certain Rich Man*, by having his hero, John Barclay, give away the "dirty dollars" that he had amassed during his lifetime. Frank Norris, after dwelling on the power and the nerve and the skill of his market operator in *The Pit*, engineered a similar last-minute conversion. And Robert Herrick caused his "American citizen," the sausage-maker Van Harrington, to think his way through to a new Darwinian competitive ethic—something which an actual Van Harrington would probably have never bothered his head about. All three of them—White, Norris and Herrick—felt constrained by their upbringing to take their eyes off the object: the industrialist, who usually felt justice and destiny to be on his side. They misinterpreted the man of destiny when they gave him the moral qualms of the brooding novelist. And the Puritan-commercial culture was paradoxically to blame for both the man of destiny and his misinterpreter. The man of destiny went forth armed with the parable of the talents and a Calvinistic conviction of divine election; as John D. Rockefeller put it, "God gave me my money"; and the novelist, who chose to accent the New Testament, couldn't believe that John D. said that with a good conscience. But John D. did say it with a good conscience. Dreiser was the first novelist to realize that. Lacking the conviction of commercial election himself, lacking also an uneasy belief that America must be squared with the New Testament, he could simply look and report and imagine.

It is true that as a young man Dreiser had his moments when he lacked the objective vision. He confesses, willingly enough, that he often yearned for the things that wealth could buy; he had an adolescent itch for gaudy clothes, for fine estates, for dinners in lobster palaces. But he soon satisfied himself that he lacked personal capacity for the sort of life that would bring him these things, and when he eventually did make money—as editor of the *Delineator* and as the author of a couple of popular successes—he used it to finance his writing, not to imitate the Pittsburgh millionaires whose antics he had studied in the nineties. His own early desires enabled him to understand the longings of Carrie and Jennie, of Cowperwood and of Clyde Griffiths; as Louis Kronenberger puts it, he has frequently used the novel to kill the thing he originally loved. Clyde Griffiths may be taken as a portrait of the young man Dreiser might have been if events had not decreed otherwise. Simply because Dreiser created Griffiths in a confessional mood, the portrait has authenticity and symbolic truth. Clyde Griffiths may not represent America in its better moments, but he represents one American aspiration, at any rate. The fact that Dreiser did not himself go the way of Clyde Griffiths, however, riddles the deterministic philosophy which the book is intended to underscore.

I have said nothing about the barbarities of Dreiser's style; there is nothing left to say about them that hasn't been said a hundred times and more. I have said nothing about the effect that Thomas Henry Huxley and Balzac had on him, for a rereading of *Dawn* convinces me that Dreiser would have come to *Sister Carrie* and *The Titan* without their aid. Nor is there anything very specific to say about Dreiser's effect on later generations of American writers. In so far as his novels served as rallying points for the critics of the genteel—Mencken, Huneker, Vance Thompson—they have helped nearly everyone from Sherwood Anderson on down to Faulkner in a very general way. Dreiser, along with David Graham Phillips, the Shaw of *Mrs. Warren's Profession,* Brieux, Emma Goldman, Freud and Mabel Dodge Luhan as *salonnière,* helped make it possible for our novelists to admit sex as an explosive element to their fictional worlds. But American writing, in the twenties, turned vigorously away from the Dreiserian conception of fiction. Fitzgerald, Lardner, Hemingway, Thornton Wilder, Elizabeth Roberts, Katherine Anne Porter, Kenneth Burke, Erskine Caldwell, Robert Cantwell—none of these believes in the power of massed detail. Nor does Dos Passos, who has sometimes been called Dreiserian in his scope. For Dos Passos's latest method is to pare his narratives to the bone; he gets his sense of profusion simply by putting four or five narratives between the same covers. Printed as an independent novel, the story of Charley Anderson, for instance, would seem a clipped, un-Dreiserian thing. As a craftsman, Dreiser has made little mark. He remains, for me, a part of an education in ideas.

EDWIN ARLINGTON ROBINSON

Malcolm Cowley

IT WAS IN OCTOBER, 1902, not long before his thirty-third birthday, that Edwin Arlington Robinson's third book of poems appeared. He counted on it to rescue him from the furnished room on West Twenty-third Street, in Manhattan, where he lived in fear of meeting his land-lord.

His first book, or rather pamphlet, had been printed at his own expense in 1896, when he was still in Gardiner, Maine, the "Tilbury Town" of his poems. The second, called *The Children of the Night,* had been issued in 1897 by one of the "vanity publishers" who earn their profits by charging authors for the privilege of having their work appear between stiff covers. Robinson was by then nearly penniless, the family fortune having trickled away in speculations by an older brother, and it was one of the poet's Harvard friends who paid for the edition of 550 copies. It received some praise from a handful of reviewers.

This third book had traveled in manuscript to six or seven publishers. One of them—Small, Maynard of Boston—had first accepted it, then withdrawn the acceptance after a change in management, but a long time had passed before it was returned to the author. Later he learned the reason why. A junior editor had left it behind in a Boston brothel, where the kind madam took charge of it until his next visit to the brothel three months afterwards. The manuscript had then resumed its travels. Finally it was to be published at the expense of the author's friends, like *Children of the Night*, but the respected house of Houghton Mifflin had agreed to distribute it, and the friends had laid plans to assure its favorable reception. Presentation copies would be sent to famous writers of the day. Various Harvard professors would be asked to review the book, and it would be priced at only a dollar to encourage a wide sale.

The author of the book was a big-framed, lean young man with a high narrow forehead, a luxuriant brown mustache and glowing brown eyes behind spectacles. He was shy and almost speechless in company until he had taken half a dozen drinks and could say, "Now I'm up where you people are." Drunk or sober he had a sense of his incapacity for practical work. "If I could have done anything else on God's green earth," he told a friend, "I never would have written poetry. There was nothing else I could do, and I had to justify my existence." He had spent years on the new book, with special attention to the title poem, "Captain Craig," which was the longest, most defiant work he had so far undertaken. With a mixture of realism, eloquence and mischief it describes the death of a pauper who is more to be admired than all the rich men of Tilbury Town. Emery Neff has the right phrase for it, in his book on Robinson, when he calls it "a two-fold assault upon conventional conceptions of beauty and conventional ideals of success." For the time when it was written, Robinson himself was not exaggerating when he called the poem "revolutionary."

But his revolution was like one of those Central American plots that end with a few shots fired and some junior lieutenants in the guardhouse. The book appeared and nothing in the literary world was changed. The presentation copies mostly went unread. The favorable reviews by Harvard professors were never written or never published, except for Trumbull Stickney's friendly lines in the *Harvard Monthly*, which appeared after a long delay. Most of the other reviews were short as well as belated; the longer ones attacked the book as a threat to ideality.

"Can the lesson be lost?" said the *Independent*. "Shall not the many merits of the book . . . rather emphasize than conceal the dangers to which poetry is exposed at present?" "Worse than Browning . . . a mistake rather than a failure," said the famous poet Bliss Carman. Then silence fell. It was as if Robinson and his friends had painfully rolled a boulder to the edge of the Grand Canyon, pushed it off and waited breathlessly. After a while there was the echo of a pebble-sized splash far below, and then they were alone in the desert.

The desert for Robinson was the fourth-story room where he sat in a rocking chair always facing the door, as if he expected someone to appear and change his life. Creaking back and forth the chair complained for him; the poet said nothing. He was tired of sending contributions to the magazines, which accepted very few of his poems and hadn't paid for one since 1895. He was tired of borrowing money from his friends. He had to refuse dinner invitations because his clothes were too shabby; often he ate his meals at the free-lunch counters of the neighborhood saloons, where he could load his plate with pig's feet after buying a schooner of beer. He looked so forlorn that once when he was eating alone at the Old Homestead, on Ninth Avenue, the waiter offered to lend him two dollars. Finally a friend almost as poor as himself offered to find him a job, and he went to work as a time-keeper for a subway construction gang, at twenty cents an hour for a ten-hour day.

He was sharing in the general defeat of almost all the serious writers who had come forward during the 1890's. Dreiser, for example, went through similar experiences at exactly the same time. Disheartened by the failure of *Sister Carrie* and by the refusal of magazine editors to print his work, he sat brooding in a furnished room like Robinson's and wondered whether he shouldn't commit suicide. His brother Paul Dresser rescued him and sent him to a sanitarium. There he was told that he should spend his days outdoors until his full recovery, and so he went to work for a railroad construction gang for $1.20 a day. Among the novelists of the time who had tried to write about American life in the naturalistic fashion, Dreiser was the only one to survive into another era. The others had either died prematurely, like Crane, Norris and Harold Frederic, or else they had gone over to the enemy like Hamlin Garland, who had been the prophet of a new American literature and who by 1900 was writing Western romances to be read in porch swings.

ii

Robinson would be almost the only survivor among the poets, and eventually he would become the lonely spokesman for a generation that had vanished. When he attended Harvard as a special student, from 1891 to 1893, the poets there had been a brilliant band which Robinson envied from a distance. Some of the names were William Vaughn Moody, Philip Savage, Hugh McCulloch, Trumbull Stickney—the most talented—and George Cabot Lodge. Santayana, another survivor, said of them when they were gone, "All these friends of mine, Stickney especially, of whom I was very fond, were visibly killed by the lack of air to breathe. People were very kind and and appreciative to them, as they were to me, but the system was deadly and they hadn't any alternative tradition (as I had) to fall back upon; and, of course, they hadn't the strength of a great intellectual hero who can stand alone." Robinson would have felt ashamed if anyone had called him an intellectual hero, but he had a single-minded devotion to poetry that was lacking in most of the others, besides a stubborn capacity to endure. If asked what he did during the bleak years for American literature after 1902, he might have given the same answer that Abbé Sieyès gave when asked what he had done during the Reign of Terror: "I lived." He lived without writing much verse, but also without betraying his ideals. During the eight months that he worked in the subway he went underground, literally, as serious American writing had figuratively gone underground.

He emerged slowly, as if he had become afraid to live in

the sun. The story of his reappearance begins late in 1903 at Groton School, where Kermit Roosevelt was then a student; he asked one of the instructors for a good book to read. The instructor, who had known Robinson in Maine, suggested *The Children of the Night*. Kermit was so impressed by it that he ordered several copies from the publisher and sent one of them to his father in the White House. The President was equally impressed; he read some of Robinson's poems aloud at a Cabinet meeting and carried the book along with him on his campaign tour that fall. "What shall we do with Robinson?" he asked Richard Watson Gilder of the *Century*, who had come to interview him on "The President as a Reader." The editor suggested a post in the consular service, but Roosevelt didn't believe that poets should live abroad. In June 1905 he made Robinson a "special agent" in the New York Custom House at a salary of two thousand dollars a year and with the understanding that he should spend his time writing poetry. It was one of the few occasions—Hawthorne's appointment to the Custom House in Salem, and later as consul at Liverpool, was another—on which an American administration has come to the aid of a talented man of letters.

Still the poetry refused to be written. Robinson was recovering very slowly from the failure of *Captain Craig*, and he was spending more time in "shopping"—as he called his nightly tour of the neighborhood saloons—than he was at his writing table. It wasn't until he lost his post in the Custom House, at the beginning of the Taft administration, that he gathered up courage to write a new book. *The Town Down the River*, as he called this group of poems chiefly about New York, was a little more conventional than his early verse and it would be more favorably reviewed. It was published by Scribner's in 1910, a year before Harper's published Dreiser's *Jennie Gerhardt*. Dreiser and Robinson never met, but they emerged from obscurity together after suffering the same defeat.

In the poetry revival that began in 1912, "the lyric year,"

Robinson played only an indirect part; he was bored by the arguments and out of sympathy with many aims of the younger poets. "Do you write free verse?" a stranger asked him, and Robinson answered, "No, I write badly enough as it is." He owed a debt, however, to the crusaders for free verse and especially to Amy Lowell, who greatly admired his work. As a result of their campaigns the magazines were printing more poems, including more of Robinson's, and the public was buying more of his books. His prospects seemed so encouraging that he stopped drinking after a long struggle, during which he told his friend Ridgely Torrence that he felt like "scratching down the stars." He also abandoned the attempt to write plays and novels on which he had wasted three years; once more he gave all his time to verse.

By 1920 the younger poets regarded him as a figure to be revered from a distance. He had two distinctions in their eyes; the first was that, in spite of the wasted years, he had devoted more time to poery than any other American and had become, except for Robert Bridges in England, the finest technician writing conventional verse in the English language, with few rivals in France or Germany. But the second distinction seemed more important: Robinson was then the only American poet who had achieved an integrated career and one that was marked by complete absorption in his art. For poetry he had sacrificed everything else: marriage, home, the respect of his neighbors and the hope of rising in the world. Poetry was his vocation, his avocation and his livelihood, such as that was, for he lived without teaching or book reviewing or lecturing or reading from his books; he simply worked and expected to be fed like Elijah by the ravens.

Actually it was his friends who fed him after he lost his post in the Custom House. They were not too rich themselves, but they clubbed together and, beginning in 1916, gave him an income of twelve hundred dollars a year, sometimes increased by special gifts; it was equivalent to the salary, at the time, of a junior instructor in a small college. Not until 1922, when he was fifty-three years old and had published his *Collected Poems,* did he become completely self-supporting. The gifts he received before that time didn't wound his Yankee pride because he felt that they were being given not to him as a person, but through him to poetry. Having taken vows of poverty, chastity and obedience to his art, he could accept donations as if he were a whole monastic order.

iii

But he paid a price for his defeats and renunciations, in his work as in his life. After the failure of *Captain Craig* he never again displayed the resilience and high spirits of that volume. His humor became a subdued irony and he lost his eagerness for making experiments. What was worse, he seems to have lost most of his intellectual curiosity. He continued to admire the authors he had read at Harvard in 1891–93 and he showed no interest in the new ideas that were sweeping over the world. One finds little trace of them, for example, in his famous philosophical poem "The Man against the Sky," written in 1915. His biographer Emery Neff says that the poem, "bringing to bear upon the supreme problem of human destiny consummate qualities of intellect, human understanding and art, towers above any other . . . written upon American soil." Does it tower above Whitman's "Song of Myself"? or above Hart Crane's "The Bridge"? or even above several of Robinson's shorter poems? To me it seems to be written with an eloquence that is not Robinson's style at its laconic best; sometimes it suggests the high fuzziness of his friend William Vaughn Moody. The consummate ideas to be found in the poem are largely complaints against scientific materialism in the forms it assumed during the 1890's:

> *Are we no greater than the noise we make*
> *Along one blind atomic pilgrimage*
> *Whereon by crass chance billeted we go*
> *Because our brains and bones and cartilage*
> *Will have it so?*

Robinson's answer is simply that we *must* have a grander destiny. For, if the materialists are right about us—

> *If there be nothing after Now,*
> *And we be nothing anyhow,*
> *And we know that,—why live?*

For himself he had first been forced and then had deliberately chosen to live obscurely and almost surreptitiously. He avoided famous persons instead of seeking them out; the company he preferred was that of his friends, and later of his disciples. He traveled only from New York to New England at the beginning of each summer and back again in the fall. He never saw the South or the West, and it was not until 1923 that he made his first trip across the Atlantic. It lasted three months and he came back without crossing the Channel, a little disappointed by the fact that he was not more widely known in England.

Having existed for years in miserable surroundings, he became indifferent to his surroundings; any room would do if it had a bed, a table and a rocking chair. From 1918 to 1922, when he could have afforded a better home, he lived in an old-fashioned railroad flat in Brooklyn. The dining-room was Robinson's study, and there he received his guests, including two poets from Harvard. He worked on a golden-oak pedestal table covered with a heavy vomit-colored cotton cloth; behind him was a built-in china closet painted a hideous brown and containing, instead of dishes, neat piles of Sweet Caporal cigarettes in pasteboard boxes. Later I learned that he lived in the flat through kindness for a boyhood friend whose wife had deserted him; but I still wondered why Robinson and the friend hadn't moved, as they could easily have done, to a less dismal lodging. The truth seems to have been that he didn't notice the objects around him and wasn't impressed by their shapes or colors.

He was cut off from any functional relationship with the community, as husband, father, employer, or employed; he wasn't even a taxpayer until the success in 1927 of his Arthurian epic *Tristram* earned him a small fortune and enabled him to pay his old debts with New England scrupulosity. He was loyal, modest, full of compassion, and yet his separation from society threw him back on himself and forced him to create characters out of his own mind. He gave them wonderful names—John Evereldown, Luke Havergal, Miniver Cheevy—and curious fates, but in his later years he sometimes forgot to give them faces. Some of the long poems that he wrote after *Tristram* are like the conversations of ghosts in unfurnished rooms. But twenty or more of the shorter poems are unforgettable, not only for their subtlety, not only for their sober diction, but also for their moments of splendor that burst like thunderstorms in the desert, as at the end of "Eros Turannos":

> *Meanwhile we do no harm; for they*
> *   That with a god have striven,*
> *Not hearing much of what we say,*
> *   Take what the god has given;*
> *Though like waves breaking it may be,*
> *Or like a changed familiar tree,*
> *Or like a stairway to the sea*
> *   Where down the blind are driven.*

UPTON SINCLAIR

Robert Cantwell

IN TERMS of his professional career, Upton Sinclair is one of the oddest and most spectacular figures in American literary history. This pale and soft-voiced ascetic, with his near-sighted smile, his disarming candor and his strangely prim and dated prewar air of good-fellowship and enthusiasm, has been involved, ever since he began to write, in knock-down and drag-out conflicts of such ferocity and ruthlessness that they might well demoralize a dozen hardened captains of industry. When you look over his career as a whole it seems to have a lot in common with those old-fashioned serials in which the hero was at the point of being pushed over the cliff or shoved into a buzz-saw at the end of every chapter, only to be preserved for greater hazards and climaxes that, oddly enough, bore no relation to those he had just escaped. Few American public figures, let alone American inspirational novelists, have written so many books, delivered so many lectures, covered so much territory, advocated so many causes or composed so many letters to the editor, got mixed up in so many scandals, been so insulted, ridiculed, spied on, tricked and left holding the bag—few, in short, have jumped so nimbly from so many frying pans into so many fires, and none has ever managed to keep so sunny and buoyant while the flames were leaping around him.

So far as I can make out, about the only really calm period in Sinclair's career was that between the mess about Eisenstein's Mexican film—with Sinclair under fire from both sides—and the outbreak of his EPIC ("End Poverty in California") campaign for the governorship. Another time, back in 1910, there were a few relatively quiet months in a single-tax colony outside Philadelphia—during them Sinclair wrote an unpublished sequel to his *Love's Pilgrimage*, was arrested for playing baseball on Sunday and fell in love with a famous suffragette, while his wife ran off with a young poet who celebrated the affair by writing a detailed account of his courtship. Aside from such pastoral interruptions, Sinclair's life has been one of incessant high-pressure executive activity, and what makes it appear fantastic and unreal is that Sinclair never seems to have been aware of this fact. In a way he belongs in the ranks of those good-hearted and unworldly eccentrics, of the type of Bronson Alcott, who had contributed so much to American culture—the starters of colonies and the believers in mental telepathy, the authors of prophetic works and the friends of cranks and faddists, the originators of diets and the apostles of nature therapy—but unlike them he has always been a man of action as well, plunging headlong into the teeming submoral atmosphere of American business and politics, with their everyday frame-ups and routine treacheries that, in business and political circles, are as completely taken for granted as the custom of shaking hands.

In his autobiography Sinclair pictures himself as a poet, a reformer, a prophet, a novelist, and writes about his naïveté with a humor and an honesty that carry conviction; but the record emerges as more puzzling and interesting. He was born in Baltimore in 1878, into an old border-state family that had been split by the Civil War and that, a decade after Appomattox, had its prosperous enterprising branch, already adjusted to the commercial order of things, as well as its genteel and demoralized representatives of defeat. Sinclair was born into its poor branch; his father was a liquor salesman who became a drunkard. The boy's early memories were of his father's periodic drunkenness and remorse, of hunting for bed-bugs in miserable hotel rooms, of dining with an aristo-

cratic grandmother, in great style, on bread and dried
herring; then of visiting rich relatives like Uncle Bland,
founder of the United States Fidelity and Guaranty
Company, or Grandfather Harden, treasurer of the Western Maryland Railway, who was recalled as a silent old
man constantly carving unending quantities of chickens,
turkeys, ducks and hams. At ten Sinclair enrolled in a
tough New York East Side grammar school. At twelve he
completed his course. At fourteen he entered City College, and before he was graduated was making his living
writing jokes for the newspapers and romances for pulp
magazines. While he was a student at Columbia, before
he was twenty, he was a full-fledged hack, with an income
of $70 a week, two secretaries, and a weekly output of
56,000 words of patriotic drivel about the Spanish-Ameri-
can War.

He was intense, nervous, chaste, easily influenced, per-
plexed about religious problems and worried about sex,
an amateur violinst who lectured his sweethearts about
venereal diseases, went on fantastic bicycle rides of a
hundred miles a day and suffered from blinding surges
of unfocused emotion that he interpreted as symptoms of
genius. At twenty-two he married and wrote his first
serious novel. In the next four years he wrote three more,
including the first volume of his unfinished Civil War
trilogy, *Manassas*. His wife was separated from him by her
parents after the birth of their son and rejoined him to
live in poverty in a house in the woods outside Princeton
—they were sick, humiliated, borrowing money and beg-
ging for subsidies, so harassed that once Sinclair, "grim
and implacable," forced his wife to return a thirty-cent
tablecloth she had purchased, and once he awakened at
night to find her with a revolver in her hand, preparing to
kill herself. They had no point of contact with their
immediate environment. Sinclair had no faith in the poor
farmers who were their neighbors; he felt sorry for them
and he understood why they were poor and demoralized,
but his essential attitude is expressed in his description of
families containing "drunkards, degenerates, mental or

physical defectives, semi-idiots, victims of tuberculosis or venereal diseases." Nor was there any companionship or strength or assistance to be drawn from middle-class friends. The smooth intellectuals from Princeton who showed up, paying attention to his wife, evidently aroused in the novelist such animosity that when he came to create the most despicable character in his works he identified him only as a Princeton man. His inspiring associations were his Socialist friends and benefactors in New York City—such people as George Herron, a former clergyman who had married a rich woman, or Gaylord Wiltshire, a retired real-estate promoter of Los Angeles—wealthy radicals who were devoting their fortunes to the movement and who, as the sports and freaks in the mutations of capitalism, have figured more prominently in Sinclair's novels than any other native type.

At twenty-eight Sinclair was a national figure with *The Jungle*. He had a fortune of $30,000, had lunched with the President, turned down an offer of $300,000 to start a packing company, and had been defeated, by the votes of the poor farmers of whose weakness he was always so powerfully aware, as a Socialist candidate for Congress. At twenty-nine he had lost most of his money in Helicon Hall and was charged with having started the fire that destroyed it, in another newspaper sensation. Thereafter his life settled to its norm of battles and scandals, breaking out in Bermuda and on Mobile Bay, in New Jersey and in a physical-culture sanitarium at Battle Creek, Michigan; in California and on Long Island—struggles over the suppression of his books; imprisonment for picketing the Rockefellers after the Ludlow Massacre; polemics at the time of the split with the Socialists when he supported the entry of the United States into the War; the scandal of the Harry Kemp–Sinclair divorce case and the sensation of his remarriage, with the disinheriting of his wife by her wealthy and reactionary Mississippi family; all building up to the Eisenstein affair and to the EPIC campaign, perhaps the single most significant development, in view of the forces supporting it and the way it was fought, in recent American political history. There was an almost perfect political symbolism in Sinclair's personal disputes. It was in the cards, given his Puritanism and his evangelical political fervor, that his household should be disrupted, not by the upholders of capitalism, but by some passing representative of bohemian irresponsibility—just as it was in the cards, in view of the inclusive, optimistic, uplift sort of socialism that Sinclair advocated, that he should first go to jail as the result of an absurd dispute with an anarchist.

Between battles and during them the books were written, usually aimed at some specific objective, filled with contradictions and repetitions and wretched writing, beginning well and ending badly, revealing a strong narrative power unfortunately devoted to telling the same stories again and again. Sinclair's works have scarcely been seriously criticized. Van Wyck Brooks's severe judgment was based on only three of his weakest novels, and Floyd Dell's biographical essay, while interesting for its facts, was written in a period when estheticism was dominant in American literature, and is primarily devoted to establishing the social value of Sinclair's books. There are times when, bogging down in their almost abandoned sentimentality, you feel sure they are nothing if they are not socially useful. To a generation of esthetes and sophisticates their shoddy writing served as the strongest possible reason for remaining in the ivory tower; and their stock situations, stock characters, stock jokes, the obvious collision between their earnest simplifications and the complexities of the postwar world, their lack of finish and their almost gushy hippity-hop humor, served to dramatize the difficulties in the way of creating a working-class literature or even of a literature that attempted to deal squarely with political issues. Sinclair became, and all the more strongly in view of the wide international circulation of his works, the prime example for reactionary critics of a creative writer whose sensitivity to people has been blunted by his political convictions and whose standards of taste have been sacrificed for the immediate necessities of his causes. At their worst his books were the products of a radical hack, and of no greater literary consequence than the Spanish War romances he turned out by the dozen in college—that they were sincere and unaffected, and that Sinclair had almost single-handedly uncovered a great unexplored area of American life, only deepened the problem.

Sinclair's novels abound in unconscious revelations of his indifference to his craft and his lack of regard for the memory of his readers. In the middle of *Mountain City* you stumble across the same situation found in *Oil!*, except that in *Mountain City* it has almost nothing to do with the story, and the esthetic effect is about like that produced when the needle gets caught in a groove of a phonograph record. Then too, Sinclair's favorite jokes and his after-dinner illustrations of his various reforming messages keep turning up like old friends in volume after volume, until they wind up in his autobiography, where he tells where he first heard them. The plots of his novels are so devious as to call to mind those railroads that were laid out in the days of land grants and that circle all over the map to take in the power sites and the rich stands of timber—so Sinclair usually works his books around until he gets to some corruption high in the mountains of upper-class life, branching off to touch on how county officials are bribed and swinging far off his course again to introduce mental telepathy as well as the problem of a rich boy in love with a socialist lass. Many of these branch lines touch on rich natural dramatic resources, but Sinclair is usually too busy staking out the territory to exploit it carefully. Even at the end of *The Jungle*, which is his best and most deeply felt book, he went out of his way to bring in a manifesto he had once written and an advertisement for the newspaper that published the book; in the manuscript he had even reached out to Idaho to introduce the Big Bill Haywood frame-up, but he dropped it again as not having much connection.

But despite these lapses—and apart from the question

of how influential they were in fortifying a whole generation of novelists in their political indifference—the picture
of American society that emerges from Sinclair's books as
a whole is in itself an achievement of a high order. Sinclair's moral strength has never let him escape an awareness of the degradation and humiliation that are the
normal lot of the oppressed in *our* republic, and his
honesty has never let him remain silent about them. The
consciousness of writing primarily for a foreign audience—
since *The Jungle* his books have circulated abroad more
than at home, until he is probably the most widely read
American writer—has given him a sensitivity to aspects of
American life that his contemporaries have overlooked or
scorned as too ephemeral to be dignified in prose. As a
result he has recorded and explained a wide variety of
native phenomena, ranging from the ramifications of
Prohibition to the development of religious revivals in
Southern California, and capturing those commonplace
expressions of American culture that usually go unrecorded
solely because they are commonplace. In the same way he
preserved in his novels (where, in fact, they are usually
lugged in by the heels) the jokes and gossip about the
ways of millionaires and movie stars and politicians, the
stories about Harding and Coolidge and Hearst, that it
seems everyone knows too well to consider significant,
but that actually add up to an unconscious expression of
the attitudes of ordinary citizens toward their heroes and
rulers.

Indeed, it seems to me that Sinclair's major achievement lies in the preservation of such miscellaneous data
rather than in his stylized and inflexible political studies.
When he tells us how strikes are put down or sold out, or
how public officials are corrupted, or how labor spies are
planted, he is describing a formula, and with that his
interest ceases and his imagination fails to give him anything new or fresh. But when he writes of such things as
an automobile drive over the Ridge Route outside Los
Angeles, in the days before the pavement was widened,
then the musty details of road hogs and speed traps, of

stopping to put on chains for rainy weather, summon up the already vanished mood of primitive motoring and make Sinclair a new type of unpretentious social historian. The memorable parts of his books lie in such details— the exact descriptions of how pigs were killed in the Chicago stockyards in 1906, the vivid account of the drilling of the wells in *Oil!*, the picture of a Colorado mining town in *King Coal*—remaining when the hackneyed characterizations and the mechanical concept of how society is controlled have been forgotten.

Van Wyck Brooks's criticism of Sinclair's novels was that they create a mood of self-pity—that they invite a workman to feel sorry for himself rather than to develop his intelligence and study the world around him and the forms of action that are possible for him. The point is good, but it is not very relevant: Sinclair has scarcely attempted to interpret working-class life since *The Jungle*. His typical story is that of a rich young man who gets mixed up in the radical movement, and the drama lies in the dissolution of his ruling-class dogmas—the pattern of *King Coal, Roman Holiday* and *Oil!* His strongest and most original characterizations are middle-class types like Bunny's father in *Oil!* or the cranky old single-tax millionaire of *Mountain City*—people more or less akin to the George Herrons and Gaylord Wiltshires of his early days as a writer—while the miners around Hal in *King Coal,* or the oil workers around Bunny in *Oil!*, or the rank and file of the coöperative movement in *Co-Op,* serve primarily as background high-lighting the situations of the aristocrats. For a decade after *The Jungle,* Sinclair's fiction dealt almost entirely with upper-class life—in *The Metropolis, The Moneychangers, Sylvia* and *Sylvia's Marriage*—and he did not return to working-class subjects and working-class characters until he wrote *King Coal* in 1917.

Their influence is hardly more apparent in Sinclair's work than in that of his less politically conscious contemporaries. In *Oil!*, for example, Sinclair found it possible to write an exhaustive study of the industry, including a long and vivid description of how wells are drilled, without giving an account of what the oil workers themselves actually do. The limitation does not merely result in a general one-sidedness in his panorama—it accounts for a blurring of the technical descriptions and an elementary sort of vagueness in the prose. In *Roman Holiday* the same limitation is more strikingly dramatized—the young millionaire has come into direct conflict with the workers and has been responsible for the death of a working-class leader, whereupon the novel breaks in two, with its second section laid in ancient Rome and its ruling-class dilemma repeated in that antique setting.

Out of Sinclair's later works you get a definite impression that his attention is focused on the upper-class world that he usually describes with a mixture of heavy-handed satire and emotional appeals to reform itself. His imagination is filled with the intrigues and maneuvers and hypocrisies of capitalists—the exact fashion in which William Fox lost his fortune, the intricate detail behind the Teapot Dome scandal, the process by which an independent oil dealer challenges the monopolies, the limitless distortions and evasions of the newspapers, the inside stories of the Mellon distilleries in *Wet Parade,* or of Coolidge's actual behavior during the Boston police strike—almost as if he expected to find, within this mash of corruption and plotting, some secret key to the history of his time. But his exposés are never as enlightening as they promise to be, and his reiterated explanations of frame-ups and wirepulling never really explain much.

All his works of this sort came to a climax in his account of the EPIC campaign, when he was himself not only on the inside but at the very center, and so in a position to know at first hand the secrets of capitalist political control. And *I, Candidate for Governor and How I Got Licked* is a frank and conscientious record of those consequential weeks that tells everything except how Sinclair was defeated. It is filled with disclosures of what went on in hotel rooms and law offices and newspaper offices—what Westbrook Pegler said and what he wrote, what President

Roosevelt promised Sinclair and how the promise was broken, what George Creel said and what William McAdoo said and what Giannini said and what James Farley said and what Fulton Oursler said—how some crafty lawyers tried to disfranchise the unemployed supporting Sinclair and the way the plot was discovered—how Sinclair's words were distorted and where Sinclair blundered —how the *Literary Digest* poll was rigged and how Sinclair received the news of his defeat—giving an interesting picture of a political campaign from the inside and a warning of what a genuinely popular reform move is up against. But it contains no disclosures of what went on in the ramshackle halls and the rented houses where the EPIC movement grew, and no disclosures of what was going on in the minds of the masses who suddenly took political initiative out of the hands of professional politicians. Nor does it reveal what the anonymous thousands of volunteer workers said to each other as, in the space of a few months, they created a political party out of nothing, or what they said as they collected funds and held meetings and published newspapers and held together in spite of the sickening slanders in the press and the routine treacheries of the politicians—although their unstudied words might conceivably be more meaningful and interesting, as well as more deeply felt, than Roosevelt's unkept promises.

These paradoxes in Sinclair's writing and in his career are a measure of the difficulties in the task he set for himself. He is the first important American novelist to see in the struggle between capital and labor the driving force of modern industry; he has hammered away for a lifetime at the cruelties and injustices of exploitation as well as at the grossness and insensitivity of life among the exploiters, and his books, with all their unevenness and vacillations, have a simple literal honesty about them that makes the work of most of his contemporaries seem evasive and affected. He has done more than any other American novelist toward breaking the path for a full and realistic treatment of working-class life in fiction—the battles he has been engaged in, the enemies he has attracted and the silence and persecution with which his books have been met being his personal cost for that pioneering work. In his concern with the moral aspects of exploitation, his strong religious feeling, his indifference to Marxian theory, his reformism and his hope for a peaceful solution of the class struggle, he has been the outstanding literary representative of the Second International, in the way that a writer of the type of André Malraux—intense, defiant, scornful—promises now to become the voice in fiction of the hard-pressed and violent life of the Third.

WILLA CATHER

Lionel Trilling

IN 1922 Willa Cather wrote an essay called "The Novel Démeublé" in which she pleaded for a movement to throw the "furniture" out of the novel—to get rid, that is, of all the social fact that Balzac and other realists had felt to be so necessary for the understanding of modern character. "Are the banking system and the Stock Exchange worth being written about at all?" Miss Cather asked, and she replied that they were not. Among the things which had no "proper place in imaginative art"— because they cluttered the scene and prevented the free play of the emotions—Miss Cather spoke of the factory and the whole realm of "physical sensation." Obviously, this essay was the rationale of a method which Miss Cather had partly anticipated in her early novels and which she fully developed a decade later in *Shadows on the Rock*. And it is no less obvious that this technical method is not merely a literary manner but the expression of a point of view toward which Miss Cather had always been moving—with results that, to many of her readers, can only indicate the subtle failure of her admirable talent.

If we say that Miss Cather has gone down to defeat before the actualities of American life, we put her in such interesting company that the indictment is no very terrible one. For a history of American literature must be, in Whitman's phrase, a series of "vivas for those who have failed." In our literature there are perhaps fewer completely satisfying books and certainly fewer integrated careers than there are interesting canons of work and significant life stories. Something in American life seems to prevent the perfection of success while it produces a fascinating kind of search or struggle, usually unavailing, which we may observe again and again in the collected works and in the biographies of our writers.

In this recurrent but heroic defeat, the life of the American writer parallels the life of the American pioneer. The historian of frontier literature, Professor Hazard, has pointed out that Cooper's very first presentation of Deerslayer, the type of all pioneers, shows him a nearly broken old man threatened with jail for shooting a deer, a pitiful figure overwhelmed by the tides of commerce and speculation. In short, to a keen observer, the pioneer's defeat was apparent even in 1823. The subsequent decades that opened fresh frontiers did not change the outcome of the struggle. Ahead of the pioneer there are always the fields of new promise, with him are the years of heartbreaking effort, behind him are the men who profit by his toil and his hope. Miss Cather's whole body of work is the attempt to accommodate and assimilate her perception of the pioneer's failure. Reared on a Nebraska farm, she saw the personal and cultural defeat at first hand. Her forebears had marched westward to the new horizons; her own work is a march back toward the spiritual East— toward all that is the antithesis of the pioneer's individualism and innovation, toward authority and permanence, toward Rome itself.

ii

The pioneer, as seen by a sophisticated intelligence like Miss Cather's, stands in double jeopardy: he faces both the danger of failure and the danger of success. "A pioneer . . . should be able to enjoy the idea of things more than the things themselves," Miss Cather says; disaster comes when an idea becomes an actuality. From *O Pioneers!* to *The Professor's House*, Miss Cather's novels portray the results of the pioneer's defeat, both in the thwarted pettiness to which he is condemned by his material failures and in the callous insensitivity produced by his material success. "The world is little, people are little, human life is little," says Thea Kronborg's derelict music teacher in *The Song of the Lark*. "There is only one big thing—desire." When there is no longer the opportunity for effective desire, the pioneer is doomed. But already in Miss Cather's Nebraska youth the opportunities for effective desire had largely been removed: the frontier had been closed.

A *Lost Lady*, Miss Cather's most explicit treatment of the passing of the old order, is the central work of her career. Far from being the delicate minor book it is often called, it is probably her most muscular story, for it derives power from the grandeur of its theme. Miss Cather shares the American belief in the tonic moral quality of the pioneer's life; with the passing of the frontier she conceives that a great source of fortitude has been lost. Depending on a very exact manipulation of symbols, the point of *A Lost Lady* (reminiscent of Henry James's *The Sacred Fount*) is that the delicacy and charm of Marian Forrester spring not from herself, but from the moral strength of her pioneer husband. Heavy, slow, not intelligent, Forrester is one of those men who, in his own words, "dreamed the railroads across the mountains." He shares the knightly virtues which Miss Cather unquestioningly ascribes to the early settlers; "impractical to the point of magnificence," he is one of those who could "conquer but not hold." He is defeated by the men of the new money interests who "never risked anything"— and the perdition of the lost lady proceeds in the degree that she withdraws from her husband in favor of one of the sordid new men, until she finds her final degradation in the arms of an upstart vulgarian.

But though the best of the pioneer ideal is defeated by alien forces, the ideal itself, Miss Cather sees, is really an insufficient one. In her first considerable novel, *O Pioneers!*, she already wrote in an elegiac mood and with the sense that the old ideal was not enough. Alexandra Bergson, with her warm simplicity, her resourcefulness and shrewd courage, is the essence of the pioneering virtues, but she is distinguished above her neighbors because she feels that, if she is to work at all, she must believe that the world is wider than her cornfields. Her pride is not that she has triumphed over the soil, but that she has made her youngest brother, "a personality apart from the soil." The pioneer, having reached his goal at the horizons of the earth, must look to the horizons of the spirit.

The disappearance of the old frontier left Miss Cather with a heritage of the virtues in which she had been bred, but with the necessity of finding a new object for them. Looking for the new frontier, she found it in the mind. From the world of failure which she portrayed so savagely in "A Wagner Matinée" and "The Sculptor's Funeral," and from the world of fat prosperity of *One of Ours*, she could flee to the world of art; for in art one may desire illimitably. And if, conceivably, one may fail—Miss Cather's artists never do—it is still only as an artist that one may be the eternal pioneer, concerned always with "the idea of things." Thea Kronborg, of the breed of Alexandra Bergson, turns all the old energy, bogged down in mediocrity, toward music. Miss Cather rhapsodizes for her: "O eagle of eagles! Endeavor, achievement, desire, glorious striving of human art."

But art is not the only, or a sufficient, salvation from the débâcle of pioneer culture. For some vestige of the old striving after new worlds which cannot be gratified seems to spread a poison through the American soul, making it thin and unsubstantial, unable to find peace and solidity. A foreigner says to Claude Wheeler of *One of Ours*, "You Americans are always looking for something outside yourselves to warm you up, and it is no way to do. In old countries, where not very much can happen to us, we know that, and we learn to make the most of things." And with the artists, Miss Cather puts those gentle spirits who have learned to make the most of things—Neighbor Rosicky, Augusta and, preëminently, My Ántonia. Momentarily betrayed by the later developments of the frontier, Ántonia at last fulfills herself in child-bearing and a busy household, expressing her "relish for life, not overdelicate but invigorating."

Indeed, "making the most of things" becomes even more important to Miss Cather than the eternal striving of art. For, she implies, in our civilization even the best ideals are bound to corruption. *The Professor's House* is the novel in which she brings the failure of the pioneer spirit into the wider field of American life. Lame as it is, it epitomizes as well as any novel of our time the disgust with life which so many sensitive Americans feel, which makes them dream of their preadolescent integration and innocent community with nature, speculate on the "release from effort" and the "eternal solitude" of death, and eventually reconcile themselves to a life "without delight." Three stories of betrayal are interwoven in this novel: the success of Professor St. Peter's history of the Spanish explorers, which tears him away from the frontier of his uncomfortable and ugly old study to set him up in an elegant but stifling new home; the sale to a foreign collector of the dead Tom Outland's Indian relics, which had made his spiritual heritage; and the commercialization of Outland's scientific discovery with its subsequent corruption of the Professor's charming family. With all of life contaminated by the rotting of admirable desires, only Augusta, the unquesting and unquestioning German Catholic seamstress, stands secure and sound.

Not the pioneering philosophy alone, but the whole poetic romanticism of the nineteenth century had been suffused with the belief that the struggle rather than the prize was admirable, that a man's reach should exceed his grasp, or what's a heaven for? Having seen the insufficiency of this philosophy Miss Cather must find another in which the goal shall be more than the search. She finds it, expectably enough, in religion. The Catholicism to which she turns is a Catholicism of culture, not of doctrine. The ideal of unremitting search, it may be said, is essentially a Protestant notion; Catholic thought tends to repudiate the ineffable and to seek the sharply defined. The quest for Moby Dick, that dangerous beast, is Protestant; the Catholic tradition selects what it can make immediate and tangible in symbol, and Miss Cather turns to the way of life that "makes the most of things," to the old settled cultures. She attaches a mystical significance to the ritual of the ordered life, to the niceties of cookery, to the supernal virtues of *things* themselves—sherry, or lettuce, or "these coppers, big and little, these brooms and clouts and brushes," which are the tools for making life itself. And with a religious ideal one may safely be a pioneer. The two priests of *Death Comes for the Archbishop* are pioneers; they happen to be successful in their enterprise, but they could not have been frustrated, Miss Cather implies, because the worth of their goal is indisputable.

From the first of her novels the Church had occupied a special and gracious place in Willa Cather's mind. She now thinks with increasing eloquence of its permanence and certainty and of "the universal human yearning for something permanent, enduring, without shadow of change." The Rock becomes her often repeated symbol: "the rock, when one comes to think of it, was the utmost expression of human need." For the Church seems to offer the possibility of satisfying that appealing definition of human happiness which Miss Cather had made as far back as *My Ántonia*—"to be dissolved in something complete and great . . . to become a part of something entire, whether it is sun and air, goodness and knowledge."

It is toward that dissolvement that Miss Cather is always striving. She achieves it with the "sun and air"— and perhaps few modern writers have been so successful with landscape. She can find it in goodness and in society —but only if they have the feudal constriction of the old Quebec of *Shadows on the Rock*. Nothing in modern life, no possibility, no hope, offers it to her. She conceives, as she says in the prefatory note to her volume of essays, *Not Under Forty*, that the world "broke in two in 1922 or thereabouts," and she numbers herself among the "backward," unaware that even so self-conscious and defiant a rejection of her own time must make her talent increasingly irrelevant and tangential—for any time.

iii

"The early pioneer was an individualist and a seeker after the undiscovered," says F. J. Turner, "but he did not understand the richness and complexity of life as a whole." Though Miss Cather in all her work has recognized this lack of understanding of complexity and wholeness, and has attempted to transcend it, she ends, ironically enough, in a fancier but no less restricted provincialism than the one she sought to escape. For the "spirituality" of Miss Cather's latest books consists chiefly of an irritated exclusion of those elements of modern life with which she will not cope. The particular affirmation of the verities which Miss Cather makes requires that the "furniture" be thrown out, that the social and political facts be disregarded; the spiritual life cannot support the intrusion of all the facts the mind can supply. The unspeakable Joseph Joubert, the extreme type of the academic verity-seeker, says in one of his *pensées*: " 'I'm hungry, I'm cold, help me!' Here is material for a good deed but not for a good work of art." Miss Cather, too, is irked by the intrusion of "physical sensations" in the novel. And one remembers Joubert's hatred of energy—he believed that it hindered the good life and scorned Balzac for his superabundant endowment of it—and one sees what is so irksome in Miss Cather's conception of ordered living: it is her implied praise of devitalization. She can recognize the energy of assiduous duty but not the energy of mind and emotion. Her order is not the channeling of insurgent human forces but their absence.

We use the word "escape" too lightly, no doubt; when we think how each generation must create its own past for the purposes of its own present, we must realize that the return to a past way of thought or of life may be the relevant criticism of the present. The only question, then, is the ends such criticism serves. Henry Adams's turn to the twelfth century was the attempt to answer the complex questions of the *Education* and to discover a better direction of energy; Eugene O'Neill's movement toward Catholic theology, crude as it may seem, has the profound interest of an energetic response to confusion. But Miss Cather's turn to the ideals of a vanished time is the weary response to weariness, to that devitalization of spirit which she so brilliantly describes in the story of Professor St. Peter. It is a weariness which comes not merely from defeat but from an exacerbated sense of personal isolation and from the narrowing of all life to the individual's sensitivities, with the resulting loss of the objectivity that can draw strength from seeking the causes of things. But it is exactly Miss Cather's point that the Lucretian *rerum natura* means little; an admirer of Virgil, she is content with the *lacrimae rerum*, the tears for things.

Miss Cather's later books are pervaded by the air of a brooding ancient wisdom, but if we examine her mystical concern with pots and pans, it does not seem much more than an oblique defense of gentility or very far from the gaudy domesticity of bourgeois accumulation glorified in the *Woman's Home Companion*. And with it goes a culture-snobbery and even a caste-snobbery. The Willa Cather of the older days shared the old racial democracy of the West. It is strange to find the Willa Cather of the present talking about "the adopted American," the young man of German, Jewish or Scandinavian descent who can never appreciate Sarah Orne Jewett and for whom American English can never be more than a means of communicating ideas: "It is surface speech: he clicks the words out as a bank clerk clicks out silver when you ask for change. For him the language has no emotional roots." This is indeed the gentility of Katherine Fullerton Gerould, and in large part the result, one suspects, of what Parrington calls "the inferiority complex of the frontier mind before the old and established."

Yet the place to look for the whole implications of a writer's philosophy is in the esthetic of his work. *Lucy Gayheart* shows to the full the effect of Miss Cather's point of view. It has always been a personal failure of her talent that prevented her from involving her people in truly dramatic relations with each other. (Her women, for example, always stand in the mother or daughter relation to men; they are never truly lovers.) But at least once upon a time her people were involved in a dramatic relation with themselves or with their environments, whereas now *Lucy Gayheart* has not even this involvement. Environment does not exist, fate springs from nothing save chance; the characters are unattached to anything save their dreams. The novel has been *démeublé* indeed; but life without its furniture is strangely bare.

VAN WYCK BROOKS

Bernard Smith

IN 1936 Van Wyck Brooks was fifty years old. We think of it with some uneasiness. We have grown so accustomed to identifying him with the younger men who have carried on the work he began and the critical spirit he initiated, that we are astonished to learn he has actually lived through half a century. At the same time, we find it remarkable that the man who has so profoundly influenced a whole generation of critics is *only* fifty. Perhaps our sudden realization that he is both older than we thought and younger than he should be, is the real measure of his position in American letters.

It was in 1915 that his voice, powerful despite its gentleness, urbanity and patience, became significant in the councils of criticism. In a volume entitled *America's Coming-of-Age*, he made certain observations on American literature and asked certain questions about the future of American culture that were startling to a people habitually determined upon treasuring the former and saluting the latter. He was not the first to trouble the waters. Before him there had been Boyesen, Peck, Pollard, Spingarn, Huneker and, above all, the *Masses* group led by Floyd Dell. In their different ways and in greater or lesser degree, each had contributed to the intellectual ferment that threatened to destroy the community's values in the realm of art. But Brooks was not a "foreigner," not a Catholic, not a Jew, not a Westerner, not a radical, not even simply a New Yorker corrupted by those alien influences. He was a Yankee of Protestant descent who had been graduated from Harvard. That was the important thing. He was a native, brought up in the traditional home of our dearest literary heritage. Its past was in his bones, its spirit was his spirit, yet he turned against it. His turning was not merely a skirmish; he was not satisfied with picking inadequacies and pointing to desirable adventures. He wrestled with the whole of American culture, with its literature and philosophy and their relation to the society they came from, and he did so in the very language of his subject. *His* conclusions, ironical, subtly contemptuous, but ultimately inspiring, could not be repudiated on the ground that he was incapable of understanding the things he dealt with.

He was a brilliant youth, but *America's Coming-of-Age* was not an immaculate conception. He had plowed the ground for its growth. Seven years before, he had published a little book called *The Wine of the Puritans* in which he had examined (although without arriving at a final decision) some of the issues that became his lifelong preoccupation. Then had come his studies of Symonds and Wells and a collection of essays on European writers, three books in which he dwelt upon figures who were products of a richer, older and presumably freer civilization than ours, yet whose lives illuminated the problems *we* faced. When Brooks turned again to the mind of his own country, he knew exactly what he wanted.

As a practicing critic, he wanted more than anything else a great literature made "out of American life"—a literature that would constitute the soul of his people, at once born of the race's spiritual experiences and upholding those experiences for the race to live by. Only Whitman, of the classics, could be accepted in the light of such an ideal, he said. In all the others—Hawthorne, Irving, Bryant, Longfellow, Emerson, Lowell, Poe—"something has always been wanting . . . a certain density, weight and richness, a certain poignancy, a 'something far more deeply interfused,' is simply not there."

Having said so much, Brooks went deeper—to the

civilization which created that literature. (For literary criticism, he said elsewhere, "is always impelled sooner or later to become social criticism . . . because the future of our literature and art depends upon the wholesale reconstruction of a social life all the elements of which are as if united in a sort of conspiracy against the growth and freedom of the spirit.") And about that civilization, that way of thought, he could say little or nothing that might flatter the intellectual jingoes. He wrote: "From the beginning we find two main currents in the American mind—both equally unsocial: on the one hand, the transcendental current, originating in the piety of the Puritans, becoming a philosophy in Jonathan Edwards, passing through Emerson, producing the fastidious refinement and aloofness of the chief American writers, and resulting in the final unreality of most contemporary culture; and on the other hand the current of catch-penny opportunism, originating in the practical shifts of Puritan life, becoming a philosophy in Franklin, passing through the American humorists, and resulting in the atmosphere of our contemporary business life."

It was true in its time, and utterly damning, and it was sufficient to make his book extremely important. But not even then was his thesis complete, for he was courageous enough to confront the end of his reasoning and honest enough to state it. Since it was the American mind, American culture, society, that was the source of our failures and frustrations in literature, it was necessary to put forth a new social ideal—one "that shall work upon us as the sun acts upon a photographic plate, that shall work as a magnet upon all these energies which are on the point of being released"—an ideal that would fuse matter and spirit into an "organic whole." Simply and briefly, self-fulfilment as an ideal had to be substituted for self-assertion. "On the economic plane, this implies socialism; on every other plane it implies something which a majority of Americans in our day certainly do not possess —an object in living."

But this, after all, is an old and rather dull story, you

may say. Precisely: and because you have said it you have shown how deeply his theory has penetrated into our literary thinking. It was not an old story when he first told it. Leon Kellner's history of American literature was published that same year (1915); Mencken's essay on "Puritanism as a Literary Force," in A *Book of Prefaces*, was not published until 1917; Waldo Frank's *Our America* was published in 1919. Consider again the points made by Mr. Brooks in the course of his argument: America's esthetic taste, after a hundred and fifty years, was still immature, its *belles lettres* still afflicted with pernicious anemia; the reasons for these conditions lay in the Puritan and pioneer traditions, the springs of an excessively utilitarian and commercial environment; the artist could function in that environment only by escaping to an ethereal private world or by conforming to the artifices and duplicities of convention, neither of which was a happy choice; and no other way out existed than the way toward collectivism.

Now, it is not my contention that any of these points was "original" or "revolutionary." The utilitarian character of American life was damned for its strangling effect upon our literature many times by many writers in the nineteenth century; indeed, a glance in that direction was made as long ago as 1799 by Charles Brockden Brown. Certainly the union in one man of an interest in an application of literary and social criticism was not unique: William Dean Howells, to take an obvious example, had occasionally approximated it. Nor was he alone in his belief in socialism as the prerequisite of a great art in the twentieth century: Upton Sinclair had said the same thing before and Floyd Dell was saying it now and saying it better, more persistently, and more vigorously. But who before Brooks, in a study of American literature and culture, had united all those elements so clearly, cogently and persuasively? And who else, in the years just before and during the World War, had so accurately keyed the pitch of his argument to the *Zeitgeist*?

The time was the Wilsonian era, the period of the

"New Freedom," when one could justly say, as Brooks himself said, that "a fresh and more sensitive emotion seems to be running up and down the old Yankee backbone." In the space of a brief essay it is difficult to describe the scene. But surely the reader will recall that the rise of finance capitalism had been accompanied by the rise of a strong labor movement; that the spreading psychology of imperialism following the war with Spain had been balanced by a growing social idealism; that urbanization, wealth, leisure and contact with recent intellectual movements in Europe had hastened the disappearance of provincialism and the bourgeois prudery misnamed Puritanism; and that consequently many developments that were pleasant, even exhilarating, to intelligent and cultivated people had been stimulated—notably, a renaissance in poetry, a new militancy in feminism and a rather curious acceptance of the Socialist Party in respectable circles. It need hardly be demonstrated that Mr. Brooks's work was a perfect and glowing expression, in criticism, of the temper of those years.

To say that he fitted his age is in no way to detract from his accomplishment. It is to say only that the age was ready for him, for his sentiments were such as belong to rebels and idealists always. The particular ideas in which his sentiments were embodied could not have exercised so great an influence before then, but they have since become the *minimum* platform of liberal and radical writers, who, it happens, have consistently formed the "younger" generation of critics. In a sense, he had nothing more to say, except to refine, strengthen and at last systematize his principles. In one respect he had overstated his position: the American literature of that time was not really so barren as he would have had us believe. Dreiser had already published his masterpieces; Henry James had not yet fallen silent. In another respect he had understated it: the broad tendencies he described and judged were too generalized and inclusive. The history of American society is not a simple, continuous line, but a complex of conflicts, tensions and resulting progressions. It was essential that Mr. Brooks analyze the charted streams into their obscure but definitely separate currents in order to clarify the points of agreement and disagreement between diverse groups of artists and philosophers in the past as well as the present. Otherwise he might be accused of distorting a reality that was damnable enough without distortions.

ii

If we may be allowed for a moment to project the experience of the 1930's into 1918, we may see at once that his next book, *Letters and Leadership*, was not quite the work anticipated. It was unquestionably a brilliant performance; it is probably the most effective piece of writing he has yet given us. But it marked an advance in style, not thought, in polish, not analysis. It did neither of the two things it should have done: it did not dig into the subsoil of American history, in which might lie the completed explanation of the contradictions in our cultural evolution, nor did it apply Mr. Brooks's known point of view to the writings of living men, which might explain the value and destination of contemporary thought. It referred to Dreiser and the *Spoon River Anthology* of Masters only to use them as illustrations of the gracelessness and cruelty of American life—references that tended to overlook the vast creative energy and the rebellious outlook inherent in both men. It castigated More, Babbitt and Brownell, but failed to place them, failed to interpret them. For the rest, it was an enlarged and bolder treatment of the residual theme of *America's Coming-of-Age*, a study of the hollowness of our literature, the shapelessness of our culture, the grossness of our life. There was but one additional note: a new emphasis on "leadership," on the need for "a race of artists, profound and sincere," who would bring us "face to face with our own experience and set working in that experience the leaven of the highest culture. For it is exalted desires that give their validity to revolutions, and exalted desires take form only in exalted souls."

It was a superlative statement of the liberal idealist's

philosophy. Its impassioned call for a "collective spiritual life" was both humane and eloquent, and its eloquence was all the more remarkable in that the author's delicate, lucid prose managed also to be firm and incisive. To be sure, that hint of distortion we found in the previous book was here too, aggravated perhaps by Mr. Brooks's insistence that artists inspire men to find salvation "from within," but there was so much truth in the sermon, so much gravity in the plea, that such objections would have seemed picayune if they had been made.

Ours is hindsight, of course, but the fact remains that they would not have been picayune. To look inward in the search for either origins or solutions of social and cultural phenomena is apparently fatal. In the public, not the private, world reside the forces whereby a community's cultural pattern may be altered. The will of the individual derives its authority from the needs of masses, not from a personal vision of the Good and Beautiful. It was Mr. Brooks's error that he pondered overmuch on the brute strength of men as compared with the frailties of man. By so doing he came gradually, no doubt unconsciously, to concentrate upon the effort required of the individual to lift himself out of the morass. This in turn led him to an acutely sorrowful pity for the artist in his tragic dilemma. We are now, I believe, discussing an attitude that is downright unhealthy for a social critic.

iii

In an essay on "The Literary Life in America," published in 1921, the reader may find some indications of the change in Brooks. It put forth nothing substantially different from the burden of the two books we have just examined; the difference was solely one of tone. The piece was tinged with despair, its apparently defiant conclusion speaking not for the nation but for the few sensitive intellectuals who retained an urge to independent creative activity. We may grant that there was ample reason for despair if we pause to recall what America was like in the years 1918–21. The Wilson catastrophe, the horrible vulgarity of Babbitt triumphant and prosperous, the Red hunts and the steel strike—these must have left their mark on him. Justified or not, however, I submit that he was yielding to an unfortunate emotion.

We saw it functioning in *The Ordeal of Mark Twain* the year before, and again, and more intensely, in 1925 in *The Pilgrimage of Henry James*. It is unnecessary to elaborate on the themes of these biographical critiques. They are well known, they have been written about frequently. In essence they are applications of his familiar thesis to the study of single writers. It was his notion that both were frustrated by the American environment. Twain stayed at home and compromised with the conventions and tastes of the "gilded age," and hence lost his soul. He suppressed the best in himself, suffered, grew embittered and even impotent. In another environment he would have been one of the great satirists of all time. James, on the other hand, fled to Europe, "and the uprooting withered and wasted his genius." The moral, in brief, is that the artist is inevitably thwarted by American life, directly if he stays here, indirectly (by losing the nourishment to be gotten from one's own soil) if he departs.

It is difficult nowadays to deny that there was a palpable distortion of reality in these biographies. Bernard De Voto's *Mark Twain's America* has convinced most of us that Twain was exactly what he was meant to be. Whatever else De Voto's book contains, it demonstrates that Huck Finn's creator was *not* frustrated and that what genius he possessed found expression. He wrote numerous bad books because that was the kind of mind and background he had, and his two or three excellent books were also written because of that mind and background. If he had been different he would not have been Mark Twain. In short, Mr. Brooks exaggerated his potentialities. As for James, no one can prove anything, yet recent treatises have made us thoroughly dissatisfied with Mr. Brooks's theory. Crucial questions are still unanswered. Was James, after all, untrue to himself? Was he so American in character that he had to wither through absence from America? Was he not a cosmopolite from his youth? And did he not, on the whole, write what he wanted to write? In short, Mr. Brooks minimized James's achievements.

Here we see the consequence of introspection upon his esthetic judgments as well as his social interests. His attention was shifting from the latter, his mood warping (no matter how minutely) the former. In the Twain book we read that "an environment as coercive as ours" obliges us "to endow it with the majesty of destiny itself in order to save our own faces"! In the James book we perceive Mr. Brooks lamenting over the fate of the first novelist "to present the plight of the highly personalized human being in the primitive community." Introspection is an indispensable critical instrument. The critic can discover the meaning and effect of a work of art only in himself, but he can give his discoveries the weight of universality and the aura of truth only by holding them to the light of historical social values. To slight the second process is to slight the rail of science that parallels the rail of poetry in the line of criticism. It is therefore not surprising that Mr. Brooks's prose was no longer "firm and incisive." It was elegiac. Softness is evident on every page of the book on James. Waldo Frank complained once of "a petulant delight in pain."

Pain, sorrow, despair—they are seldom permanent. Sometimes from their distillation comes the impersonal passion by which prophets are seized. More often what comes out of them is the calm, lightly melancholy adjustment that is akin to resignation. There is no other way to describe Brooks's *Life of Emerson* (1932). It was intended to complement the James and Twain studies in so far as it would portray an American writer who neither compromised nor fled, yet was able to live in joy and harmony with his environment. It was not, however, a critical or a psychological or a social study. It was a recreation of Emerson's life in his own words. How, then, could it give us the truth about Emerson's world and his place in it? The reader who puts it down thinking it has enabled him to understand Emerson is mistaken.

From our point of view, the implications of this revery —for that is what the book is—bear exclusively upon Brooks's relation to the critical movement of which he was the father. He had now no relation to it whatever, except a reminiscent one. That this is a continuing phase is proved by his most recent book, *The Flowering of New England*. It is composed in the same manner and the same temper as the Emerson "biography." The writing is superb, the images it evokes are memorable; in many ways it is the finest portrayal ever made of the artistic and intellectual life of New England's "golden age." But it is wholly lacking in analysis. It explains nothing, neither causes nor consequences, and therefore it truly estimates neither the significance of the "flowering" nor its ultimate value. It is purely description and narrative, and it indicates that its author has turned to scholarly storytelling. If he finds peace and pleasure in so doing, we must be glad, for no man deserves them more, and we must voice quietly our regret that he is not still an inspiring leader.

Today the position he has occupied in modern criticism is sufficiently clear to warrant our "fixing" him for future historians. He has been the most influential critic of the past twenty years. His early work was the principal factor in the erection of the lofty cultural standards that have encouraged the rise of a mature, serious, philosophical criticism. The effect of his later work was not so praiseworthy, for it led to the embittered subjectivity of such books as Lewis Mumford's *Melville* and Matthew Josephson's *Portrait of the Artist as American*. (Both men, by the way, have since rejected that mood.) In any event, for good or bad, something of Brooks has seeped into almost every American critic under fifty (including even the Marxist, Granville Hicks). There is no better testimony to his fine mind, his exquisite taste, his integrity and unselfishness. That he has taken to blaming "human nature in general" for the faults he formerly and correctly attributed to society is not (as it usually is) a sign of egotism, but a result of his withdrawal from the battle. No man ever wanted less for himself and more for his fellow men.

CARL SANDBURG

Newton Arvin

A LITTLE MORE THAN twenty years have gone by since
Carl Sandburg became known as a poet to the generality
of American readers, and now one looks back over his
career with a kind of esteem that only a few of his contemporaries inspire. In the interests of criticism several
things may have to be said about his writings in their
actual execution, but so long as you have your mind on
the main intention of Sandburg's books or the spirit in
which they have mostly been written, you are bound—
unless that intention and that spirit are too alien to you—
to take pleasure in his work and to hope that it will have
a long line of offspring. There are cases in which a fine
intention patiently and faithfully adhered to becomes itself a production to estimate and respect, and in that
sense Carl Sandburg's continuous effort to find a poetic
outlet for the fast, hard, noisy, smoky, machine-ridden
experience of Middle Western city people and for the dry,
unshaded experience of Middle Western villagers and
farmers—his effort, I say, has taken on the dimensions of a
literary achievement, and one that no disparagement can
minimize. In a generation in which most poets set themselves more manageable and more opportune tasks, he
undertook to be the poet of a people among whom the
sources of poetry, though by no means exhausted, were
untapped, grown over, and all but completely forgotten.

He was not content, unlike most poets of that generation, to explore and exploit the tortuous reaches of a

highly private and often abstruse experience, or to work out the forms of expression for a complicated sensibility—aims which, even after more than a century, still promised the most certain results to writers who worked within the romantic-individualist tradition. Sandburg's was the intention of a rhapsode or scop or (with important differences) of a younger political poet; and it led him to the attempt to get into verse the whole disorderly and humid life of the twentieth-century United States, with its violence, its grandiosity, its social tensions, and its waste of human impulse and power. He has described himself officially as an American folk song recitalist, and obviously enough the impetus behind the great bulk of his work has been to provide a minstrelsy for Chicago and Kalamazoo; for the mechanic, the typist and the farmhand. If Mr. C. H. Compton, the St. Louis librarian who reported on popular reading habits, is to be believed, Sandburg has succeeded in speaking for such people—as readers, specifically—far more fully than it would be easy and conventional to assume.

Under all the circumstances, however—circumstances of time and social condition—there was something honorably quixotic and something paradoxical in his attempting to fill this ancient or anticipatory role. The chances are that Sandburg himself has been well aware of the paradox: he once remarked to an interviewer that "saying 'Chicago' and 'poems' close together like that is like saying 'hell roses' or 'hell lilies.'" At any rate, it is certainly true that he was not very lucky in his milieu and his moment. The relation between a reflective and highly organized modern poet and the great mass of middle-class or working-class Americans could not actually be the relation between a folk-poet and his people; could not be spontaneous, intimate, many-sided and unreserved. The creator of a lay or a ballad is nourished by the life of the community about him because he can share it unselfconsciously on every level; can enter not only into the physical experiences of his people at work and play, into their sentiments and general emotions, but into their thought, their imagination and their spiritual experience. A poet of Sandburg's time and place might share, as he has certainly done, many of the simpler aspects of his people's life; but if he were a man of fine talent and serious purposes, he could not really identify himself, heart and mind, with the social world of which he was a part. There might be, as the proletarian poets have been showing, another relation and a fruitful one into which he might consciously enter; but just that was never Sandburg's clear choice, and the result has been that his environing culture has not nourished him and his poetry as they deserved to be nourished.

Thanks to the genuineness of his gifts and perhaps to some deep resource of health and sanity, he made himself a remarkable writer in spite of Chicago and Kalamazoo. But to reread his books at this hour is to see how little he has owed—how much too little—to a common way of life, a common morality, a common fund of ideas and convictions. Sandburg has not aimed, needless to say, at being a metaphysical poet, but like all writers he has evidently felt the need to discern some meaning in the welter of things and events, and the need has mainly gone unanswered. Like Dreiser, like Masters, like Anderson, he has been able to mirror—often with startling fidelity—the world about him: he has not been able to focus or integrate it. A troubled skepticism, an enervating indecisiveness, overlie much of what he has written: whenever the raw fact or the strong primitive sentiment is left behind, we are likely to find ourselves in a chartless prairie of bewilderment and doubt, with little to fix our eyes upon but a riddle or a question-mark. "Mist," "fog," "phantoms," "ashes," "dust," these are favorite images, and they are the true emblems of the poet's almost unrelieved uncertainty. Obsessed with the grimly impersonal drift of time, he has often failed to see any understandable tendency in the whole course of human experience:

> *History is no sure thing to bet on.*
> *History is a box of tricks with a lost key.*

More than once he has fallen back on a helpless relativism and a philosophy of pure chance:

> God is Luck: Luck is God: we are all bones the High Thrower rolled: some are two spots, some are double sixes.

And in the poem about the Grand Canyon:

> each one makes his own Canyon
> before he comes, each one brings
> and carries away his own Canyon—
> who knows? and how do I know?

Behind so dubious a state of mind as this lie certainly the too easy beliefs or the vulgar unbelief of our harried and leaderless population: out of that state of mind must have sprung the surprisingly harsh despondency that came more and more to prevail in Sandburg's work after the first volume and that led him, in *Good Morning, America*, to speak of "the short miserable pilgrimage of mankind" between an ice age far in the past and an ice age perhaps not so far in the future. Certainly the winds that blow across his city streets and his open prairies seem often to have reached them after passing over some near and menacing glacier. It is extraordinary, considering the warm and genial temperament that the evidence forces us to believe in, how little heat one actually finds in the pages of Sandburg's books. Of tenderness, of humane feeling, of generous and robust sentiment, there is notoriously a great deal: of strong, sharp and ardent emotion, of the specific passion and intensity of poetry, there is singularly little. This verse, you feel, is the work of a man whose emotional nature, like his intellectual life, has never found the earth and air in which it could develop freely and expansively. His strength has lain in his closeness to the people, but they are a people whose impulses and affections have been nipped and stunted like trees in a city park or like wild flowers on a stock farm; and of so cramped an emotional existence this frequently too cool, too inexpansive, too phlegmatic poetry—this poetry of

half-lights and understatement and ironic anticlimaxes—
is the inevitable expression.

In form and language it has of course reflected the intellectual perplexity and the emotional constraint that have
been its setting. Diffused through half a dozen books
there is the fruit of much thoughtfulness, much pondering,
much sensitive perception and understanding; but, with
admirable exceptions, it *is* all diffused, and not con-
centrated: in a score of poems it is unmistakable; in single
poems it is rarely fused and final. The frequent looseness
of the form corresponds to the indeterminateness of the
mental structure beneath it; and if the rhythms are sometimes broken and prosaic, the images sometimes whim-
sical or merely customary, the words themselves sometimes naked and inexpressive, it is because they have not
passed through the lens of heightened and translucent
emotion. Sandburg's words, it is true, have often come to
him from the inexhaustible reservoirs of American slang;
and, given his purpose, that was just where they should
have come from: with no other language could he ever
have rendered the surfaces or even the spirit of contemporary life as he has rendered them with his "galoots," his
"necktie parties," his "fadeaways" and his "fake passes."
But slang is an instrument with a big end and a little end,
and if one of its uses is to magnify and clarify perceptions,
another is to dwarf and blur and weaken them: it is as
often prompted by a distrust of ideas, of strong emotion
and of beauty, as by quick intelligence and fresh feeling.
It has sometimes been a decoy to Sandburg as to certain
other writers: it has led him to fritter away his meanings
instead of pointing and pressing them.

He has not, in short, made by any means so full a use of
his manifest gifts as under better circumstances he might
have made; but in spite of the pedants who prefer the perfect achievement of a modest or trifling intention to the
imperfect achievement of an ambitious or difficult one,
his qualified success has been far more impressive than the
less qualified—and lesser—successes of some of his contemporaries. This son of an immigrant Swede railroad

worker, this ex-housepainter, ex-dishwasher, ex-newspaper man, has done more than all but two or three other writers of his time to keep somewhat open and unclogged the channels that ought to flow between the lives at the base of society and the literary consciousness. The substance of his poetic insights and sympathies may be scattered rather loosely through *Chicago Poems* and *Smoke and Steel, Abraham Lincoln: The Prairie Years* and, now, *The People, Yes*; but at least it is ever present in those books, and it is not easy to think of another writer who has perceived more subtly or reproduced more variously that world of towering silos and pregnant-looking cornfields, of band concerts on July evenings and lighted ice-cream parlors, of stockyards and crowded street-cars and night skies lurid over the din of rolling-mills. The eye of a reporter-poet and the ear of a born musician have contributed their large share toward making Sandburg's books what they are.

His eye and his ear, however, have not been deserted by more essential faculties, and *The People, Yes* reminds us that, whatever his confusions and his negations may have been, Carl Sandburg's intuitive grasp of a few basic values, human and social, has never been more than intermittently relaxed. His earliest poetry drew much of its color and its lift from Sandburg's affiliation with the Socialist movement in the Middle West in the years just before the War; and even in the extreme doldrums of the twenties, his wise, homely, tender book on Lincoln showed that his imagination could not wander far from the democratic center of the American folk tradition. How generously the imagination of an American poet can be fed and the art of such a poet mellowed by that tradition, *The People, Yes*, in spite of some air pockets, amply demonstrates. In the midst of sharper and sharper conflicts between the principle of subordination and the principle of equality, this poem is an eloquent and sometimes a passionate reassertion of the dignity, the fortitude, the unweariable creativeness, the historic and unrelinquished hopes of "the laboring many." It is not, after all, as a short and miserable pilgrimage merely that Sandburg now sees the difficult record of the race:

> *And man the stumbler and finder, goes on,*
> *man the dreamer of deep dreams,*
> *man the shaper and maker,*
> *man the answerer.*

Like one of his own fogs, Sandburg's doubts and apprehensions seem to have burned off at last, and his latest words are again in the strong and sanguine spirit of his inheritance from Whitman:

> *And across the bitter years and the howling winters*
> *the deathless dream will be the stronger,*
> *the dream of equity will win.*

SHERWOOD ANDERSON

Robert Morss Lovett

A REVALUATION of Sherwood Anderson must necessarily take account of the extraordinary impact that he made upon American literature almost at his appearance. In spite of the crudity of his first novels the impression was general that an original and distinguished talent was to be reckoned with. This recognition extended to European critics, among whom Bernard Faÿ committed himself to the statement in the *Revue de Paris:* "I believe that Sherwood Anderson is one of the greatest writers of the contemporary world, and the best in America." This verdict may be accounted for by Anderson's possession, in truer balance than any other of his contemporaries, of three qualities marked by Maeterlinck as requisites for great literature: a sure touch upon the world of our senses; a profound intimation of the mystery that surrounds this island of our consciousness; and the literary technique comprehended in the term style.

I first met Sherwood Anderson in 1913 at Ernestine Evans' studio in Chicago, whither he came to read a manuscript. He was in housepainter's clothes, and seemed the proletarian writer for whom we were already on the lookout. His writing suggested Dreiser. It was minutely naturalistic, but of anything beyond this present scene, anything of grace of style, I now recall no trace. Floyd Dell, then literary editor of the *Chicago Post,* who lent his august presence to the occasion, saw with his usual discernment the promise in this attempt, and, I understand, recommended *Windy McPherson's Son* to John Lane in London, where it was received as a genuine American document. This it undoubtedly is in its first part, its substance drawn from Anderson's early life in the Middle West, but as in more than one of his novels, the point at which realism gives way to badly conceived romance is easily marked. The same verdict falls upon Anderson's second novel, *Marching Men*. In the latter, however, there is an imaginative effort to transcend the actual, to embody the significance of the great union symbolized by the march of the toilers. Already Anderson was writing the poetry which appeared the next year in *Mid-American Chants*, and infusing his prose with the soaring rhythms that carry his fiction at times into a realm in which realistic criticism is irrelevant.

Winesburg, Ohio, in 1919, marks an important date in American literary history, and in itself profited by an obvious timeliness. It was the year after the War, and readers stupefied by tales of its abominations needed to be reassured that peace hath its horrors no less worthy of renown. D. H. Lawrence had discovered sex as a source of incongruity of character. Katherine Mansfield had developed after Chekhov the story in which nothing happens but a sudden moment of illumination and awareness. The stream-of-consciousness method was a recent invention. Edgar Lee Masters in *The Spoon River Anthology* had assembled a community of people whose confessions revealed the deep places of human experience hidden by their provincial lives.

In *Winesburg, Ohio* Anderson shows perfect command of the small-town stuff familiar to him from his youth. True, he protests:

> I myself remember with what a shock I heard people say that *Winesburg, Ohio* was an exact picture of Ohio village life. The book was written in a crowded tenement district of Chicago. The hint for almost every character was taken from my fellow lodgers in a crowded rooming house, many of whom had never lived in a village.

Nevertheless, they live there now. In the process of transference from the crowded rooming house into an environment which Anderson controlled so completely that the reader takes it for granted, they have assumed an actuality that is not dependent on realism. They move among the material furnishings of the world with the deftness and precision of sleepwalkers. If Anderson had left them in their rooming house he might have written another *Pot-Bouille*. Instead he has made a character sketch of the rotten little town which has become as much a part of the American scene as Gopher Prairie or Muncie, Indiana. As a literary form, a group of tales adding up to a unit greater than the sum of its parts, the book is a masterpiece. Mr. Cleveland B. Chase in his rather disparaging brochure on Anderson admits that it is "one of the most important products of the American literary renaissance, and has influenced writing in America more than any book published in the last decade."

Winesburg, Ohio represents the solution of the problem that Anderson consciously set himself. His own experience, unusually rich and varied, gave him his grip on the actual world in which he was to live so abundantly. He has borne testimony to this in his numerous autobiographical writings, but as an artist his aim was constantly to emerge from the chrysalis stage of realism into the winged career of imagination. "Imagination must feed upon reality or starve" is a sentence from his notes which in effect recurs again and again. Of the process of transubstantiation he gives an explicit account in *A Story-Teller's Story*. As a boy he listened to his father, a fantastic liar who had served in the Civil War and on the basis of that fact made himself the hero of a dozen campaigns to the delight of his audience. Sherwood inherited or learned the knack. "When I was a lad," he tells us, "I played with such fanciful scenes as other boys played with brightly colored marbles. From the beginning there have been, as opposed to my actual life, these grotesque fancies. Later, to be sure, I did acquire more or less skill in bringing them more and more closely into the world of the actual."

In so doing he worked at this relation of material to imagination, and the projection of fact into fiction. Humble and sordid realities, the trivia of observed phenomena, bring to him an emotion which is the essence of poetry. In *A Story-Teller's Story* he recalls such a moment of inspiration. Looking from a window, he sees a man in the next yard picking bugs off potato vines. The man's wife comes to the door, scolding. He has forgotten to bring home the sugar. A quarrel follows. And for Anderson his own life and interests, his business and his waiting dinner, are forgotten. "A man and a woman in a garden have become the center of a universe about which it seemed to me I might think and feel in joy and wonder forever." It is in thus seizing on scraps of reality and projecting them beyond the small range controlled by the senses that Sherwood Anderson's imagination brings fiction to the enhancement of life, and enlarges his art beyond the limits of naturalism into expressionism. Not the fact, but the emotion with which the artist accepts it, is the essence of living.

Winesburg, Ohio is not only an instance of the evolution of a literary theory; it marks also Anderson's achievement of a craftsmanship which is an essential part of that theory. When in his preface to *The Triumph of the Egg* he speaks of himself as a tailor, "weaving warm cloth out of the thread of thought" to clothe the tales which, born of experience and imagination, "are freezing on the doorstep of the house of my mind," he is using a figure that comes naturally to him. He was an artisan before he was an artist. His work as sign painter and mechanic gave him a sense of the relation of materials and tools. As a tailor of tales he finds excitement in pen or pencil and paper, thousands of sheets of it, waiting for his hand. The author's medium is words, which are to him what pigments are to the painter, or food stuffs to the cook. One of his happiest sketches is that of Gertrude Stein bustling genially about her kitchen choosing the ingredients of her pastry. From her, it may be conjectured, Anderson gained something of the assurance that words have qualities inherent in them other than meaning. "Words have color, smell; one may sometimes feel them with the fingers as one touches the cheek of a child." It is through words that the experience of men and women in the actual world is communicated and shared.

For the communication of the immediate scene Sherwood Anderson has mastered his instrument. But, as he repeatedly asserts, mere realism is bad art. His peculiar quality resides in his intuition of something behind the scene, something "far more deeply interfused" whose dwelling is not for him "the light of setting suns" but rather "the mind of man." As Mr. Boynton remarks: "Anderson did not hit on this true note of his own until he reached the point where he became more interested in what was happening in the minds of his individuals than in what was going on outside their bodies." It is in states of consciousness which eventuate in moments when the unconscious wells up and overwhelms personality with a sense of completion in the larger unity of life that his creative power resides, and it is with such moments that his characteristic stories deal. A recurring theme in them is the effort of the character to break down the wall which confines the individual in isolation from this general life which he shares with his fellows. Sometimes this theme comes to explicit utterance, as in "The Man in the Brown Coat":

> I'll tell you what—sometimes the whole life of this world floats in a human face in my mind. The unconscious face of the world stops and stands still before me.
> Why do I not say a word out of myself to the others? Why, in all our life together, have I never been able to reach through the wall to my wife? Already I have written three hundred, four hundred thousand words. Are there no words that lead into life? Some day I shall speak to myself. Some day I shall make a testament unto myself.

Naturally in this pursuit of unity, in this breaking down of separateness, Anderson is much concerned with human relations and especially with sex. Through sex is maintained the great flow of the race of which each individual is but a drop. Sexual intercourse seems the most hopeful point of assault upon the wall which keeps each individual a prisoner. "The Egg," in his second series of tales, is concerned with a desperate effort of a broken man to preserve some sort of human relationship through the performance of a trick, but the title gives an ironical significance to the volume—*The Triumph of the Egg.* Nearly all the stories are concerned with sex, from the boy's view of its mystery in "I Want to Know Why," to the tragedies of frustration in "Seeds," "Unlighted Lamps," "The Door of the Trap," "Out of Nowhere into Nothing." It is worth while to mention them, for each is a triumph, a witness to Anderson's mastery of the short-story form. The next series, *Horses and Men,* continued the theme in "Unused."

Anderson's later novels bear an increasingly definite relation to the social scene. For him, the Middle West reveals on a large scale the restless striving, the frustration of unfulfilled purpose, which is so often the theme of individual life treated in his short stories. *Poor White* is an ambitious attempt in which, as in the earlier novels, a firmly realized conception tends to lose its way in cloudy romance. Hugh McVey is a boy in "a little hole of a town stuck on a mud bank on the western shore of the Mississippi," where he follows his father listlessly about, sweeping saloons, cleaning outhouses, or sleeping on the river bank with the smell of fish upon him, and the flies. A New England woman takes Hugh in hand and trains him, so that after her departure his awakened will forces him into sustained activity. He becomes an inventor, an industrial magnate. Like Sam McPherson and Beaut McGregor in *Marching Men,* the hero loses identity, but throughout the mass of the book the symbolism is closely woven into the realism, as warp and woof.

Hugh McVey, the physically overgrown, almost idiotic boy, is the Middle West in the last decade of the century. When by sheer strength of will he harnesses his mind to problems of mechanical invention and solves them by a power he does not understand, he typifies the spirit of industrial pioneering in all its crude force. Sarah Shepherd with her schoolmistressy formula, "Show them that you can do perfectly the task given you to do, and you will be given a chance at a larger task," is the spirit of New England brooding on the vast abyss of the Middle West and making it pregnant. Harley Parsons with his boast: "I have been with a Chinese woman, and an Italian, and with one from South America. I am going back and I am going to make a record. Before I get through I am going to be with a woman of every nationality on earth, that's what I'm going to do"—what is he but an ironic incarnation of our national destiny? Joe Wainsworth, the harness maker who in his hatred of machinery or machine-made goods kills his assistant, is the ghost of the horse-and-buggy age attacking the present. Smokey Pete, the blacksmith who shouts to the fields the scandal he dares not utter on Main Street, is the spirit of American prophecy, a Jeremiah of Ohio. Anderson has made his story a sort of Pilgrim's Progress of the Midwestern life he knows so well.

The best of Anderson's novels is undoubtedly *Dark Laughter*. It is not only a good novel in structure and movement, but more subtly than *Poor White* or *Many Marriages* it is of that thoughtful quality which entitles it to rank among the novels of ideas. The two themes which are woven together are leading ones with Anderson: freedom through craftsmanship and freedom through love. The hero, Bruce Dudley, walks out of his home and his job as a reporter and finds work in an Ohio village in Grey's carriage factory. There he meets Sponge Martin, who teaches him how to paint carriage wheels and how to live. His philosophy is that of art as a guide to life:

> Perhaps if you got the thoughts and fancies organized a little, made them work through your body, made thoughts and fancies part of yourself—they might be used then, perhaps as Sponge Martin used a brush. You might lay them on something as Sponge Martin would lay varnish on it. Suppose about one man in a million got

things organized a little. What would that mean? What would such a man be? Would he be a Napoleon? A Cæsar?

Bruce meets Aline Grey, the wife of his employer, and with her steps forth on the road to freedom. Meanwhile the Negro world which surrounds them, in its dark laughter, sounds an ironic chorus.

In his later novels Anderson has shifted his scene to the South. There the process of industrialization, going on more ruthlessly, fills him with horror. Scenes in the cotton mills recur with a kind of obsession. Rather timidly he puts forward his social remedy in *Perhaps Women*, the result of "a growing conviction that modern man is losing his ability to retain his manhood, in the face of the modern way of utilizing the machine, and that what hope there is for him lies in women." *Beyond Desire* is an expression of the two elements—sex and industry—but it can scarcely be maintained that any essential relation between them is established. *Kit Brandon* is an example of that "assisted autobiography" in which the author enters into the experience of another person, in this case a bootlegger whose career is not without social implications. In form it is evidence of Anderson's ability to enforce his claim, "I write as I like"—but the reader finds himself sighing for the lucid simplicity of *Moll Flanders*.

Recently Anderson put forth a brief statement in *Story* Magazine which emphasizes what is true of his writing at its best—that in its fact, and its imaginative penetration beyond fact, it is a phase of his experience:

> I think that writing or painting or making music . . .
> is merely a tool a man can sometimes use to get at this
> business of living. . . . It is all wrapped up in this other
> thing . . . a man's relationships . . . his handling of re-
> lationships, his striving, if you will, for the good life.
> Relationships, I should say, with the world of nature too,
> development of the eyes, ears, nose, fingers. It is even, I
> think, concerned with the way you touch things with
> your fingers.

Some years ago Anderson forsook the "solemn and perhaps even asinine business, this being what is called great, doing immortal work, influencing the younger generation, etc.," and engaged in the humble business of editing a small-town newspaper—two, in fact, for there were two in town, one Democratic and one Republican. In playing the parts appropriate to the several stock characters in the newspaper play, society reporter, sports reporter, editorial writer, etc., he found abundant opportunities for cultivating relationships and leading the good life. Whether we get masterpieces from him or not, he has given an indication of the sincerity of his profession that art is a part of experience, not something added thereto, and that an artist may be too interested in life to care overmuch about success in it.

H. L. MENCKEN

Louis Kronenberger

MENCKEN CAME IN like a lion. Like a revolutionary, over-throwing half the props that supported America's conception of itself—and not merely its beliefs and moralities, but its peace of mind. His scathing mockery of those who made our laws, our culture and our social sanctions electrified an age that had few pioneers, and no pioneer save Mencken with a loud voice. College professors, shocked at his view of life in general and insulted by his view of themselves, virtually regarded him as Antichrist. Women's clubs put off discussing him from year to year. Right-thinking business men disposed of him as a Bolshevik. But the War had produced a whole new generation, out of joint with the old traditions and hostile toward them, who were stirred by Mencken's rhetoric and ideas, and who were eager to be infected with his laughter. It suited their temper to learn from him that all our sacred cows were incredibly stupid and clumsy field beasts; to learn, for that matter, that despite what they had been taught in the past, *nothing* was sacred.

For a few years after 1918, when Mencken's influence was waxing or at its height, America was intellectually in a disobedient mood. Cheated in the War of actual scars, she managed to acquire a very convincing case of shell-shock and St. Vitus' dance, to want new and quick sensations, to practice exhibitionism under the name of defiance, and to visit death upon the timid, genteel and sanctimonious values that so long had kept her dead.

Truth might be hard to reveal, but cant was easy to expose; adjustment might be hard to come by, but repressions were easy to throw off. There was much talk and some show of liberalism, but certainly the commoner phrase and the commoner aspiration was to be "emancipated." The fraudulent nature of the War, the sharp decline in religious faith, the advancement of science, the birth of psychoanalysis, the new experimentalism in the arts, were at once the causes and the symptoms of this aspiration. There was a small group, well-informed, social-minded, political-minded, who rationally absorbed these other ideas into an attitude that had its feet on the ground and an eye to the future. But for many others, most of them immature, the ideas were chiefly a pretext for escape, for asserting one's independence and skepticism. For them the great problem was to be delivered at any cost from outworn dogmas.

Mencken lay to their hand, and they to Mencken's. He was not of the liberal camp—a pooled enterprise resting on more or less common ideas about life—but an "advanced" individualist, stemming loosely from individualists of a previous age. Among his forebears, Nietzsche was that kind of philosopher, Wagner that kind of composer, Shaw that kind of pamphleteer, Huneker that kind of critic. These men were not so much rebellious of the thinking of their day as subversive of it. They simply pushed out on the offensive. In time each exerted much influence, for a personal idiom is always more likely to exert influence than an impersonal ideology. Clearly Mencken followed in their footsteps. He had a personal idiom unmatched in his generation; it could be instantly felt; and coming at a moment when individualism on its lower levels was the gospel of American life, it was bound to command a hearing.

Mencken like the others took the offensive. For years culture in America had been standing still, corruption had been growing, and criticism on all fronts had been paralyzed by timidity and ignorance. But the War had torn off a few masks, dislodged a few certainties, given doubt and skepticism an opening. Mencken proceeded to widen and enlarge that opening enormously. Wilson's last days and Harding's brief ones, the fight over censorship, the advent of prohibition—any number of things strengthened his cause. He launched a massive attack on everything this country held inviolate, on most of what it held self-evident. He showed how our politics was dominated by time-servers and demagogues, our religion by bigots, our culture by puritans. He showed how the average citizen, both in himself and in the way he let himself be pulled round by the nose, was a boob. He burst out that the country was a desert of philistine vulgarity, and could only be looked upon at all because it was so endlessly comic. Any progress that might be attempted in the cities was blocked by envious blue-nosed "peasants" on the farm. The high priests of culture—professors and academicians—were enemies of culture. Sex was defiled by the filthy-mindedness of prudes. It was impossible, Mencken insisted, for any sensitive or civilized person to be a party to conditions so revolting; he could only laugh at them and turn away.

The upshot of this unsparing diagnosis—which in theory constituted a kind of wholesale muckraking—was not a general movement toward reform, but a special movement toward withdrawal. It fostered the cult of the civilized minority. In the thick of his blistering charges against American life in general, Mencken somehow contrived to make the individual reader feel exempt from the indictment, an *âme bien née* who belonged on the side of Mencken and the angels. Thus the situation, from the outset, was ironical. Mencken, exposing the ghastly inadequacies of all matters of public interest, encouraged his readers to be too snobbish to give a damn about them. He insisted he could offer no remedy and was amused that he should be expected to. Those whom he influenced at once accepted his conclusions, turned their backs on the national plight and set up as a civilized minority.

Most of the literature of the day moved in the same

direction. It came in two forms, each of them congenial to Mencken's teachings: satire at the expense of a stunted America, and a tony skepticism that considered life in the raw intolerable, and life in general comic. This second style of writing, as refined by the watered esthetics of Cabell, Hergesheimer, Van Vechten, Frances Newman and others, soon became mere snobbism. The first, though often in the Mencken spirit, yet had a more serious effect upon our cultural life because it was sometimes launched with more sense of protest than Mencken would have approved of. Sinclair Lewis, for example, fought now and then where Mencken never did more than egg on. But in general the satire was something to smile over to the same extent that the skepticism was something to feel uppish about. In short, if most men will act like fools, let wise men be amused by their antics.

ii

This concept, which is really the cornerstone of Mencken's thinking, is equally the index—for I shall no longer attempt to hide my bias—to his utter inadequacy. He approached his job with a keen intelligence, a wealth of facts and a superb gift for communication. But he approached it without the seriousness of a true satirist, and was content that his findings should arouse an unreflective mirth. What he liked was the noise and fun of battle. That is all right in its place, gusto and audacity are great weapons; but a real satirist will of course go farther. Even if he cannot in honesty seek to convert people to a program, at least he will seek to convert them to the necessity of finding one: to make them feel responsible, to make them care. Mencken did just the other thing. He sought to make them laugh, he labored to *épater le bourgeois*, he kidded the good along with the bad, he tried to find a common denominator of absurdity in virtually everything: finally his craving to say the unexpected wore down his integrity against saying the untrue. Charity, free education, the liberalism of college professors came in for the same pummeling as the antics of the vice-snoopers.

The tone, at length, became that of an unredeemed cynicism: the tone, not of a man who did not believe, but of a man who did not want to believe. "I have no remedy to offer," was uttered, not humbly, but smugly. Now any man worth his salt who is bitten by skeptical pessimism must feel the double responsibility of his position—must see that the more life darkens, the more imperative becomes the search for light. So a Matthew Arnold, seeking to combat in his generation many of the abuses that Mencken railed against half a century later, sweated after a solution and, forlornly pinning his hopes on Culture, drove furiously. He may have seemed a little ridiculous at times, but he never seemed cheap. Mencken, on the other hand, was no more an honest skeptic than he was an honest satirist. *Que sçais-je?* stands at the very opposite pole to the gaudy knowingness that has crept more and more into Mencken's manner. He has taken the Easiest Way of the philosopher, the least responsible way of the citizen. "If I am convinced of anything," he said in 1927, "it is that Doing Good is in bad taste." Just so Hergesheimer held that giving money to starving children in Europe was "one of the least engaging ways in which money could be spent" (if we can trust a story repeated in Emily Clark's *Innocence Abroad*); just so Cabell said, "I burn with generous indignation over this world's pigheadedness and injustice at no time whatever."

Mencken, far from leading America out of the wilderness, merely bade the elect, from some secure elevation, watch their less enlightened brethren wriggle and squirm. Nor was their security rooted in laughter alone; it was the security of the good years, of mirth begotten by prosperity, when Mencken's verbal antics stood out boldly, and his toryism did not. For in those days of our democratic inflation, his un-American brand of reaction, his own version of Nietzsche, seemed just one more instance of his striving to be perverse. Indeed if he seemed then tory at all, he seemed—in Max Beerbohm's phrase—like a tory anarchist. But Mencken's toryism never really was, and now nowhere seems, playful. He was perhaps most in earnest when he went to work against three-fourths of the ideas that all progressive systems would deem self-evident and share in common; perhaps most in earnest when, snorting at ignorant Red-baiting, he indulged in a subtler Red-baiting of his own. In a dozen books you could hardly hope to achieve what Mencken achieved merely by reiterating the phrase "poor old Debs" or by describing Marx as "a philosopher out of the gutter."

Consider briefly a few manifestations of Mencken as a reactionary—and not merely as a political reactionary. In the space of twenty pages of *Prejudices: Fifth Series* he comes out against birth control ("I believe that the ignorant should be permitted to spawn *ad libitum* that there may be a steady supply of slaves"); in defense of capital punishment; in favor of war. Elsewhere he opposes circulating the theory that crime is mostly pathology; endlessly he jeers at education; endlessly he extols the Junker system. Nor does a lifetime of ridiculing the stand-patters in art cancel out the fact that in practice Mencken much oftener ridicules novelty of expression than he endorses it. Plainly enough (and almost as plainly then as now), most of the artistic isms and movements of his day were showy frauds, and he reached the right verdict about them; but always in Mencken there was a predisposition to annihilate them on principle, and he saw no difference at all between the gifted early Stravinsky and somebody who composed a tone-poem for frigidaires. He simply hid a conservative's taste under a firebrand's vocabulary.

It was in his popularizing of a few cardinal ideas— the farcical aspects of democracy, the loutish intolerance of the "peasantry," the folly of being contaminated by the mob, the vast quackery in American life—that Mencken exerted his strongest influence; for at length there was scarcely a literate man in America who was unaware of the bold top line of Mencken's oculist-chart. But it was more precisely in his comment on books and the intellectual scene that Mencken helped to govern the American mind. The literary essays in *A Book of Prefaces* and the earlier volumes of *Prejudices,* the editorials and book reviews in the *Smart Set* and the earlier issues of the *American Mercury*, proved formidable instruments—probably the most formidable of their day—in creating literary trends and reputations. If the lower-browed Phelps could help sell a quarter-million *If Winter Comes*, the tougher-minded Mencken could help sell almost as many *Babbitts*. Almost unaided, Mencken first set the Middle Western school of fiction on its feet. Doubtless an Anderson or a Hecht would have found his market anyway, but except for Mencken I doubt whether a Ruth Suckow or a G. D. Eaton would ever have been heard of. He was of immense value also in promoting the careers of men like Hergesheimer and Cabell, writers who, using a different idiom from Mencken's, yet preached a similar view of life. Both schools that he espoused came in for a profitable run; both are bankrupt today; neither one produced any writer of first-rate talent. Sinclair Lewis and the less classifiable Scott Fitzgerald were by far Mencken's best bets among the writers coming up in his prime—for his praise of Lardner came belatedly; and among Americans of an earlier day Dreiser is perhaps the only one whom Mencken was right about and whose career he helped to establish.

Mencken's most valuable single contribution to American criticism was his fight to purge our literature of its puritanism and gentility. By jumping on the bodies of timid critics and timid novelists alike, by discrediting their flabby values and bloodless evasions, he more than any other man opened up pioneer spaces and enabled us, at least technically, to come of age. Sex ceased to be a bugaboo, squalor a tabu, decorum a virtue, iconoclasm a subversion of ethics. So far, so good. Where Mencken fell down, however, was in lacking an esthetic judgment to match his common sense. A very good pamphleteer, he turned out to be a very bad critic. Once he got into the temple of art, he seemed no better than an adventurer. He drummed up bad novelists and shouted good ones down. He called Robert Frost "a Whittier without the whiskers" and proceeded forthwith to exalt John McClure and Lizette Woodworth Reese. For poetry, of course, he notoriously had no genuine feeling at all. He is a fairly good amateur critic of music, though when he makes such statements as that the *Egmont* Overture is an aphrodisiac, one can only look blank. Quite possibly his best criticism lies in scattered remarks about men's religious, philosophical and scientific beliefs, where he is often searching and alert. But in the end we are confronted by someone who, though he touched on almost all topics in a critical spirit, was of no real consequence as a critic.

His importance, on the serious side, lies—as I have hinted—in his ability as a pamphleteer. He shattered many weak-kneed idols; he crushed the drowsy venom out of many serpents still trying to hiss in the late afternoon; he railed against thou-shalt-nots that did not make sense; he gave us some idea of how often we could be duped and fooled. If he had no true sense of the profound, he had an unfailing sense of the absurd, and that had its serious value in the pamphleteer. To the role of comedian he brought great gifts. He had an eye not only for marking out stray instances of the fatuous, but also for playing one instance against another, for shaping them into patterns, for giving them true reach and breadth. He was one of the best phrase-makers, both journalistic and literary, of his generation; and he had at his command a preternaturally bold and vivid style. His keen interest in words produced, indeed, a work so sound and fascinating as *The American Language*, which will probably outlive anything else he has written. But elsewhere, too, his prose reveals an absolutely personal idiom. Mencken had manner and will be read for his manner, at least in small draughts, a fair while after his content has gone into the rubbish heap. His style has drawbacks, of course—the greatest being that, as somebody said of Macaulay's, it is a style in which it is impossible to tell the truth.

For, like all men too fond of shocking, too intent on making a point, too desirous of seeming original, Mencken indulged in much disingenuous thinking, much cleverness; and these blemishes remain blemishes quite apart

from the abuse he made of his cynicism, the sly weapon
he made of his conservatism. To bring Mencken up to
date is only to say that most of his virtues have declined
and that all of his faults have increased. The critic in him
touched the low of a lifetime when he published his
shabby and unscrupulous essay on the proletarian school
of novelists; the tory in him went farthest right when,
during the 1936 campaign, he published his cheap word-
juggling on Roosevelt and the New Deal. In each instance
the attack was not levied on valid grounds in a critical
spirit, but was hurled on extrinsic grounds with a dema-
gogue's appeal to mob psychology. We can hardly hope
to find Mencken turning over new soil of any kind in the
future. He has come to a dead halt both in ideas and in
curiosity. He will fall back, I think, within narrower and
narrower range, upon the assumptions that have always
fathered his thinking. These are assumptions that have
long fathered the thinking, not of our best philosophers,
but of the secure and the complacent, those who when
Rome burns can escape to their villas at Baiæ. But even
the Baiæs of this world are not made of asbestos.

SINCLAIR LEWIS

Robert Cantwell

WITH SOME FIFTEEN NOVELS to his credit at the age of fifty, together with enough short stories to fill several more volumes, Sinclair Lewis stands out as the most prolific author of his generation, with the mournful exception of Upton Sinclair. It is almost the worst thing you can say about him. For although Lewis has written at least two first-rate novels, and created a dozen powerful characters, and produced half-a-hundred masterly satirical sketches scattered throughout these books—as well as adding new words to the language and popularizing, more than anybody else, a new and skeptical slant on American life—he has also turned out as much journalistic rubbish as any good novelist has signed his name to, and he has written novels so shallow and dull they would have wrecked any reputation except his own.

He has, in fact, been one of the most plunging and erratic writers in our literary history; unpredictability, waywardness, unevenness are his distinguishing characteristics, as a brooding inconclusiveness is the mark of Sherwood Anderson. He has written the best novel of American business in *Babbitt*, only to make up for it by writing the worst in *Work of Art* and adding half-a-dozen wretched *Saturday Evening Post* stories on the same subject to the bargain. He has written the sharpest parodies of the lush, rococo, euphemistic sales talk of American business life that we have, but he has also weighed down his novels with a heavy burden of unreal and exaggerated jargon, palmed off as common speech, with unfunny topical jokes, passed on as native humor, and the weight of that dated mockery grows heavier every year.

But Lewis has not only been the most uneven of American novelists; he has also been one of the most ambitious. There is an architectural symmetry in the order of the books that followed *Main Street*. Unlike his contemporaries, who seem always to have been improvising in the sequence of their work, Lewis apparently recognized a conscious program for his writing simultaneously with his recognition of his power, and seems to have driven toward its realization with something of the high-pressure intensity he has satirized so often. Where Dreiser gives the impression of having brooded, with a sort of ponderous aimlessness, over whatever lay close at hand, forever turning aside, distracted by every incidental issue; where Anderson and Vachel Lindsay, more than any of the others, were blown about in the cross-currents of American life until they were saturated with its apparently patternless variety, Lewis visualized on the strength of *Main Street* a cycle of novels comparable at least in scope to those of Zola and Balzac.

It was a spacious and inclusive project, bolder than anything an American novelist had tried to do, signalizing a final break with that narrowness of outlook which, exemplified in a thousand old-swimming-hole sentimentalities, pathetic regionalisms and phony family dilemmas, had become almost the sole driving force of American fiction. And even now, when the limitations and shortcomings of that imaginative exploration are more apparent than its freshness and originality, it is still a little breathtaking to consider the broad outlines of the work that Lewis laid out for himself, to see that he planned nothing less than a catalogue of the interwoven worlds of American society, the small towns and cities, the worlds of business, of science, of religion, of education, and eventually the worlds of labor and professional politics, working it out at a time when the shabby, optimistic, patriotic smugness of the American literary tradition—the tradition of Henry Van Dyke that, significantly, he attacked in his Nobel Prize address—still imprisoned the imaginations of so many of his contemporaries.

Lewis had a line on American society, and tenacity, if not much flexibility and resourcefulness, in following it. But more than that he had a sense of the physical variety and the cultural monotony of the country, an easy familiarity with the small towns and square cities, the real-estate developments and restricted residential areas, the small business men, the country doctors, the religious fakers, the clubwomen, the county officeholders, the village atheists and single-taxers, the schoolteachers, librarians, the windbags of the lower income groups, the crazy professors and the maddened, hyperthyroid, high-pressure salesmen—the main types of middle-class and lower-middle-class provincial society, conspicuous now because he has identified them so thoroughly. He had a grasp of these people and their environments, together with a sense of the country as a whole, where so many of his generation had nothing but an oppressed conviction of its emptiness or a dread of its rawness.

Only Vachel Lindsay and Upton Sinclair had seen so much of the country, in the elementary geographical sense of the term. Lewis had never taken any of the wild and pathetic zigzag journeys of Lindsay, dropping in on miners and hill-billies and reading poems for his supper, nor had he spent a season in the hell of the stockyards, as did Upton Sinclair, his first guide, at the beginning of a career no less extraordinary. But he had knocked around at an impressive variety of jobs before and after he was graduated from Yale in 1908—he had been a janitor in Upton Sinclair's Helicon Hall, a soda jerker, a reporter on the *San Francisco Bulletin*—which was probably, under Fremont Older in the days before his capitulation, the best paper in the country to be a reporter on—a ghost writer for Jack London and an editor, in Washington, of a magazine for the deaf; he had taken the grand cruise of his generation on a cattle boat to England and had hitch-hiked through the Middle West. He had traveled over the face of the country and, although within pretty narrow limits, up and down through its social strata. And although his first four books were hack jobs, the native experiences he had packed away were too powerful to be satisfied with evocations of the joys of a stenographer's work, or of the wisdom of picturesque and homely old folks, or of an aristocratic Eastern girl made wholesome by contact with the great West—the substance of *The Job, The Innocents* and *Free Air.* Even as hack work those books are bad. They seem to tremble with some internal explosive disgust; in a way they are like the bad jokes and stale opinions that Babbitt and his friends take refuge in at their parties, when they dare not express even a little of what is going on in their minds, lest they betray their hatred of their environments, their boredom, their thwarted desire for change.

Apparently Lewis thought at the beginning of his career that the muse could be embraced and laid aside at will, and that she would not take her revenge by addling the wits of her ravisher—at least his first books prove nothing except that he did not believe the writing of fiction demanded a writer's full energy and his deepest understanding. That implicit irresponsibility has been his greatest limitation as a novelist and the source of much of the unevenness of his work. Even the broad project mentioned above—the cycle of novels following *Main Street* —is a vision of an imaginative survey of American life such as a glorified and super-competent hack writer might conceive: a writer, that is, who thought of his writing, not in terms of its momentary inspirations and the pressure of living that played through him and upon him, but in terms of the accomplishment of a foreknown task; who thought of a novel of business, of religion, of science, as if he believed he could turn his art to any subject, regardless of how much it meant to him and how close to his heart it lay; who felt that it was within his power to "collect material" without becoming emotionally entangled in it or acting in response to what it implied. T. K. Whipple, who has written the only searching study of Lewis that

we have, has compared his attitude in studying American
society with that of a Red Indian stalking through the
land of his enemies—it is a good description, for it suggests his wariness and vigilance, the surface accuracy of
his observation, what can be called the heartlessness of his
approach, and above all his enforced detachment from
the scene he viewed and the solitary and personal basis
of his satire.

ii

Now that the scandals that attended the publication of Lewis's books have been forgotten, the outlines
of the world he created are clearer. On re-examination
that world seems in a more advanced state of decay and
disintegration than his first critics were willing to admit
—it is, as Whipple has said, a city of the dead, in which
the dead are above all determined that no one shall live.
After *Main Street* his characters were still the long-
winded, provincial, narrow-visioned old folks, the dreamy
and timid job-holders, the clerks and salesmen and doctors—with here and there a workman from the semi-
independent crafts—who figured in his first books and
were all dominated by those strange, self-satisfied, self-
possessed, jovially witless bankers and business men who
loom so large in Lewis's world. But where such characters
had been harmless and happy in the early novels, they
were now vindictive, spiteful, vaguely threatening in their
inertia and immobility.

Before the War, Lewis had written of their provincialism
as if it were a source of serenity, however its expression
might rasp on the sensibilities of the cultivated; for the
provincials and the innocents themselves, it was an insula-
tion against the cares of the world and not without its
own homely poetry and wisdom. But with *Main Street*
that provincialism was identified as an evil force, destructive not only to the Carol Kennicotts and Eric Valborgs,
to Martin Arrowsmith and Paul Reisling—it was also
poisoning the lives of those who clung to it and triumphed and, when their guards were down for a mo-

ment, were seen to be bewildered, distressed, clinging desperately to their appearance of smugness because they had nothing else to cling to. The problem of *Main Street* might have been "how much of Gopher Prairie's eleven miles of cement walk" was "made out of the tombstones of John Keatses"—but the message of *Babbitt, Arrowsmith, Elmer Gantry,* however Lewis might deny that it was his intention to preach it, was simply that American society was death to any disinterested effort, to any human tolerance, almost to any human sympathy; that it was regimented within an inch of its intellectual life; that any deviation from its norm of self-seeking, money-grubbing, career-making, throat-cutting, treachery, slander, blackmailing, was instantly punished with exile and disgrace; that spontaneity or generous emotions or a freedom from calculation, among the calculating wolves of business, amounted to suicide of a long-drawn-out and painful kind. Lewis drew a revolutionary picture of American middle-class life without coming to revolutionary conclusions about it, unlike Upton Sinclair, who leaped to revolutionary conclusions and then filled in the picture; he recognized the mechanics of capitalist control, and satirized them, without challenging the ends to which they were applied or visualizing any alternative except an escape—for those sensitive souls enlightened enough to be aware of their horror—into reverie and daydreaming.

The moral atmosphere, with exceptions that will be noted, grew thicker and more poisonous with each succeeding book. Carol Kennicott's sensibilities were outraged by Gopher Prairie, and she was revolted by the hypocrisy and narrowness she found there, but the enemies she faced were largely passive—inertia, sluggishness and sullenness, the dominance of petrified prejudice. In comparison with *Babbitt* and the books that followed it, this is an almost pastoral view of life. The difference is not only in the greater violence of the later books, the general strike that interrupts *Babbitt* midway, the flare of melodrama in Reisling's attempt to murder his wife, the corruption and blackmail that accompany Babbitt's business career. It is rather in the cagey watchfulness with which Babbitt's friends of the service clubs bear down on each other for every deviation from their class line, and it is nowhere better dramatized than in the sequence that follows Reisling's tragedy—when Babbitt, shaken by it, develops an intermittent sort of tolerance, the others, particularly the sinister Virgil Gunch, get their knives ready for him at once, and the high point of the book, perhaps the highest point of Lewis's writing, is the realization that they are ready to spring, like the stronger wolves on a crippled member of the pack, at the first sign of Babbitt's confusion and dismay.

Yet even Babbitt's sacrifices for the good opinion of such prosperous thugs are nothing compared with the desperation of Angus Duer, in *Arrowsmith,* who tries to cut the throat of a watchman who has inadvertently threatened his career, and the indifference that Carol Kennicott faced in Gopher Prairie is nothing compared with the sustained enmity and malice that Arrowsmith faces in Wheatsylvania. The enemy—the provincial, conforming, suspicious enemy—is no longer merely passive and mocking; it has become aggressive, strident, criminal; it turns to blackmail and violence; it is ready to frame and destroy anyone who even raises questions that it cannot answer. And by the time *It Can't Happen Here* was written, Lewis's picture of the world was such that the violence with which the book is filled had become obsessive and perverse, divorced from any purpose and uncontrolled by any aim, an eruption of cruelty and horror and little more.

Spaced unevenly between the works in which this panorama of social damnation is drawn are those books of Lewis's that even his acquiescent critics usually overlook: *Mantrap, The Trail of the Hawk, Work of Art, Ann Vickers, Dodsworth,* the grotesque short stories that he wrote for the *Saturday Evening Post* and that seem particularly bad because there is so much evidence that Lewis knew so much better when he wrote them.

He has never been a fastidious writer—he has a gift for slogans, a talent for mimicry, a kind of tormented delight in some of the cruder commonplaces of American speech, but he has always manipulated his people awkwardly to make them demonstrate what he wanted them to reveal about society, and his works have always been weakened, even in their moments of gravity, by a tumultuous and slapstick humor that seems less an expression of emotion than of a desire to escape it. As his career has developed he has relied more and more on his ability to capture the perishable local color of American life, the blaring and raucous Babbittry that surrounds his people, the pep-talks, the idiot drooling of advertisers and go-getters, instead of the indefinite but still sustained and consequential conflicts of Carol and her husband, of Babbitt and his friends—but this material, which was used in *Main Street* to show what a character who could not stomach it was up against, began to be used in the novels that followed almost for its own sake, until with *The Man Who Knew Coolidge* there was scarcely anything else in the book.

But precisely because Lewis has attached so little fundamental importance to such outpourings as Dr. Pickerbaugh's health sermons or Chum Frinkley's poems, his increasing insistence on material of this sort is all the more clearly a sign of imaginative indecision and doubt. And how, after having so clearly shown the mechanics of American business control in *Babbitt*, and the psychological ravages of it, could he have drawn so unrealistic a figure of a millionaire as Dodsworth, or so romantic a business man as the Ora Weagle of *Work of Art?* In his best books Lewis had told us that the pursuit of wealth—or even a career in a business-dominated society—was a fierce and scrambling affair that killed its victims and crippled its victors; now he presented an industrialist whose unaccountable naïveté persisted (although he collected secret reports on the dissipations of his employees), and a starry-eyed, well meaning hotel manager whose poetic dreams revolved around the creation of more elaborate comforts for the exhausted Babbitts who could afford them—presented without art, without irony, at best with a kind of curdled romanticism that gave an impression of spleen and exasperation on the part of their author. With these books Lewis's explorations into American society stopped. His characters had become idealizations of the Babbitts he had previously condemned; his satire had degenerated to a kind of stylized mockery, closer in spirit to George Ade's *Fables in Slang* or to some of Mencken's less purposeful buffoonery than to the realities of American life—or it had become so broad and farcical that it had lost its point, just as, in his anti-fascist novel, his fascists were presented as so weird and unearthly that no practicing strikebreakers, vigilantes, lynchers, antisemites, jingoes or acquiescent journalists need feel an instant's identification with them.

iii

But with all this acknowledged, the positive contribution of Lewis's novels remains—and, in one sense, if books like *Dodsworth*, *Work of Art* or *Ann Vickers* seem so shallow, it is in large part because Lewis himself has made us conscious in his best work of the native realities that are absent in them. In his best books he has caught, better than anybody else, the desultory, inhibited, half-sad and half-contented middle-class life of the Middle West, a life of spiritless conflicts and drives in the country, of social gatherings as nerve-racking and exhausting as final examinations, of interminable business plots and fears of ruin, of frightened infidelities, limitless ambitions, of forced enthusiasms and false simplicities—a life hedged in behind social barriers set by the least enlightened members of the community and existing under a dictatorship that is no less powerful for being masked and unadmitted by those who bow to it. And even in his worst books Lewis has always been able to summon up some neglected, recognizable corner of the country—the run-down, red-leather hotel lobbies of *Work of Art*, the formaldehyde, oiled-floor, civil-service stench of public buildings in *Ann*

Vickers—with such graphic power that he has always seemed to be setting the stage for some more momentous drama than he has even shown taking place.

That effect may be the result of his inability clearly to imagine any antagonist capable of sustained struggle with the rulers of his city of the dead. He is more aware of the monstrous extent of the stables that must be cleaned than he is of the possibility of any Hercules ever cleaning them; and when he pictures people who are pitted against their environments he usually shows them struggling without much hope of victory, without allies, and often with ingrown doubts as to whether or not they are on the right side. And most often, when their feeble feints establish the strength of the enemy, they merely subside into that outward acquiescence and inward rebellion that is the death of drama—so Carol Kennicott, defeated in Gopher Prairie, dreams of a grass hut over some tropical river bank; Babbitt hungers for some wild woodland spirit as he awakens into the steel world of Zenith; Ora Weagle plans gigantic and flawless super-hotels as he fires the help of a run-down Florida boarding house, and these vague aspirations to escape their own environments are presented by Lewis as conferring some secret distinction on the people who hold them.

In denying that he is a satirist Lewis has said that he is a romantic, in much the same sense that these characters of his are romantics, and that he has rebelled against American society because it has none of the picturesque feudal remains that he associated with a rich and stable culture. But his characters are not romantic rebels committed to struggle. They are self-dramatists whose imaginations flower from their evasions of conflict—they are always posing before themselves and others, not in order to fulfill a consistent Byronic role, and to take the responsibility for it, but in order to conceal their true reactions and to hide the concerns that oppress them. They are always in the camp of their enemies; they cannot forget themselves for a moment, lest they reveal the depths of their revulsion. They dramatize themselves in order to endure the demands of a society that they have no hope of bettering and whose reality they cannot face, and they imagine themselves in all kinds of roles—except the ones they actually occupy—because they cannot get through their days without the help of such fantasy.

So the final testimony of Lewis's novels always seems a little grimmer than he apparently intended it to be, and never so grim as when he envisions the rebels and aspiring spirits who front the resolute conformists. He never comes so close to giving a clinical description of psychic breakdown as when he shows his characters making their peace with the world. It was a mistake of his critics to see in these novels evidence of that intellectual awakening and skeptical self-criticism which has become known as America's coming-of-age. For Lewis is the historian of America's catastrophic going-to-pieces—or at least of the going-to-pieces of her middle class—with no remedy to offer for the decline that he records; and he has dramatized the process of disintegration, as well as his own dilemma, in the outlines of his novels, in the progress of his characters, and sometimes, and most painfully, in the lapses of taste and precision that periodically weaken the structure of his prose.

EUGENE O'NEILL

Lionel Trilling

WHATEVER IS UNCLEAR about Eugene O'Neill, one thing
is certainly clear—his genius. We do not like the word
nowadays, feeling that it is one of the blurb words of
criticism. We demand that literature be a guide to life,
and when we do that we put genius into a second place,
for genius assures us of nothing but itself. Yet when we
stress the actionable conclusions of an artist's work, we
are too likely to forget the power of genius itself, quite
apart from its conclusions. The spectacle of the human
mind in action is vivifying; the explorer need discover
nothing so long as he has adventured. Energy, scope,
courage—these may be admirable in themselves. And in
the end these are often what endure best. The ideas expressed by works of the imagination may be built into the
social fabric and taken for granted; or they may be rejected; or they may be outgrown. But the force of their
utterance comes to us over millennia. We do not read
Sophocles or Æschylus for the right answer; we read them
for the force with which they represent life and attack its
moral complexity. In O'Neill, despite the many failures of
his art and thought, this force is inescapable.

But a writer's contemporary audience is inevitably
more interested in the truth of his content than in the
force of its expression; and O'Neill himself has always
been ready to declare his own ideological preoccupation.
His early admirers—and their lack of seriousness is a re-
proach to American criticism—were inclined to insist that

O'Neill's content was unimportant as compared to his purely literary interest and that he injured his art when he tried to think. But the appearance of *Days Without End* has made perfectly clear the existence of an organic and progressive unity of thought in all O'Neill's work and has brought it into the critical range of the two groups whose own thought is most sharply formulated, the Catholic and the Communist. Both discovered what O'Neill had frequently announced, the religious nature of all his effort.

Not only has O'Neill tried to encompass more of life than most American writers of his time but, almost alone among them, he has persistently tried to *solve* it. When we understand this we understand that his stage devices are no fortuitous technique; his masks and abstractions, his double personalities, his drum beats and engine rhythms are the integral and necessary expression of his temper of mind and the task it set itself. Realism is uncongenial to that mind and that task, and it is not in realistic plays like *Anna Christie* and *The Straw*, but rather in such plays as *The Hairy Ape, Lazarus Laughed* and *The Great God Brown*, where he is explaining the world in parable, symbol and myth, that O'Neill is most creative. His interest is not the minutiæ of life, not its feel and color and smell, not its nuance and humor, but its "great inscrutable forces." Hence the bathos and redundancy of his language, for a temperamental insensitivity to the accurate word and the exact rhythm is encouraged by the requirements of his enterprise; the search for finality tempts him toward the big and inexact words. He is always moving toward the finality which philosophy sometimes, and religion always, promise. Life and death, good and evil, spirit and flesh, male and female, the all and the one, Anthony and Dionysius—O'Neill's is a world of these antithetical absolutes such as religion rather than philosophy conceives, a world of pluses and minuses; and his literary effort is an algebraic attempt to solve the equations.

ii

In one of O'Neill's earliest one-act plays, the now unprocurable *Fog*, a Poet, a Business Man and a Woman with a Dead Child, shipwrecked and adrift in an open boat, have made fast to an iceberg. When they hear the whistle of a steamer, the Business Man's impulse is to call for help, but the Poet prevents him lest the steamer be wrecked on the fog-hidden berg. But a searching party picks up the castaways and the rescuers explain that they had been guided to the spot by a child's cries; the Child, however, has been dead a whole day. This little play is a crude sketch of the moral world that O'Neill is to exploit. He is to give an ever increasing importance to the mystical implications of the Dead Child, but his earliest concern is with the struggle between the Poet and the Business Man.

It is, of course, a struggle as old as morality, especially interesting to Europe all through its industrial nineteenth century, and it was now engaging America in the second decade of its twentieth. A conscious artistic movement had raised its head to declare irreconcilable strife between the creative and the possessive ideal. O'Neill was an integral part—indeed, he became the very symbol—of that Provincetown group which represented the growing rebellion of the American intellectual against a business civilization. In 1914 his revolt was simple and socialistic; in a poem in the *Call* he urged the workers of the world not to fight, asking them if they wished to "bleed and groan—for Guggenheim" and "give your lives—for Standard Oil." By 1917 his feeling against business had become symbolized and personal. "My soul is a submarine," he said in a poem in the *Masses*:

> *My aspirations are torpedoes.*
> *I will hide unseen*
> *Beneath the surface of life*
> *Watching for ships,*
> *Dull, heavy-laden merchant ships,*
> *Rust-eaten, grimy galleons of commerce*

Wallowing with obese assurance,
Too sluggish to fear or wonder,
Mocked by the laughter of the waves
And the spit of disdainful spray.

I will destroy them
Because the sea is beautiful.

The ships against which O'Neill directed his torpedoes were the cultural keels laid in the yards of American business and their hulls were first to be torn by artistic realism. Although we now see the often gross sentimentality of the *S.S. Glencairn* plays and remember with O'Neill's own misgiving the vaudeville success of *In the Zone*, we cannot forget that, at the time, the showing of a forecastle on the American stage was indeed something of a torpedo. Not, it is true, into the sides of Guggenheim and Standard Oil, but of the little people who wallowed complacently in their wake.

But O'Neill, not content with staggering middle-class complacency by a representation of how the other half lives, undertook to scrutinize the moral life of the middle class and dramatized the actual struggle between Poet and Business Man. In his first long play, *Beyond the Horizon*, the dreamer destroys his life by sacrificing his dream to domesticity; and the practical creator, the farmer, destroys his by turning from wheat-raising to wheat-gambling. It is a conflict O'Neill is to exploit again and again. Sometimes, as in *Ile* or *Gold*, the lust for gain transcends itself and becomes almost a creative ideal, but always its sordid origin makes it destructive. To O'Neill the acquisitive man, kindly and insensitive, practical and immature, became a danger to life and one that he never left off attacking.

But it developed, strangely, that the American middle class had no strong objection to being attacked and torpedoed; it seemed willing to be sunk for the insurance that was paid in a new strange coin. The middle class found that it consisted of two halves, bourgeoisie and booboisie. The booboisie might remain on the ship, but the bourgeoisie could, if it would, take refuge on the submarine. Mencken and Nathan, who sponsored the O'Neill torpedoes, never attacked the middle class but only its boobyhood. Boobish and sophisticated: these were the two categories of art; spiritual freedom could be bought at the price of finding *Jurgen* profound. And so, while the booboisie prosecuted *Desire Under the Elms*, the bourgeoisie swelled the subscription lists of the Provincetown Playhouse and helped the Washington Square Players to grow into the Theatre Guild. An increasingly respectable audience awarded O'Neill no less than three Pulitzer prizes, the medal of the American Academy of Arts and Sciences, a Yale Doctorate of Letters and finally, in 1936, the Nobel Prize.

O'Neill did not win his worldly success by the slightest compromise of sincerity. Indeed, his charm consisted in his very integrity and hieratic earnestness. His position changed, not absolutely, but relatively to his audience, which was now the literate middle class caught up with the intellectual middle class. O'Neill was no longer a submarine; he had become a physician of souls. Beneath his iconoclasm his audience sensed reassurance.

The middle class is now in such literary disrepute that a writer's ability to please it is taken as the visible mark of an internal rottenness. But the middle class is people; prick them and they bleed, and whoever speaks sincerely to and for flesh and blood deserves respect. O'Neill's force derives in large part from the force of the moral and psychical upheaval of the middle class; it wanted certain of its taboos broken and O'Neill broke them. He was the Dion Anthony to its William Brown; Brown loved Dion: this love was a way of repenting for his own spiritual clumsiness.

Whoever writes sincerely about the middle class must consider the nature and the danger of the morality of "ideals," those phosphorescent remnants of a dead religion with which the middle class meets the world. This had been Ibsen's great theme, and now O'Neill undertook to investigate for America the destructive power of the ideal—not merely the sordid ideal of the Business Man but even the "idealistic" ideal of the Poet. The Freudian psychology was being discussed and O'Neill dramatized its simpler aspects in *Diff'rent* to show the effects of the repression of life. Let the ideal of chastity repress the vital forces, he was saying, and from this fine girl you will get a filthy harridan. The modern life of false ideals crushes the affirmative and creative nature of man; Pan, forbidden the light and warmth of the sun, grows "sensitive and self-conscious and proud and revengeful"—becomes the sneering Mephistophelean mask of Dion.

The important word is *self-conscious,* for "ideals" are part of the "cheating gestures which constitute the vanity of personality." "Life is all right if you let it alone," says Cybel, the Earth Mother of *The Great God Brown.* But the poet of *Welded* cannot let it alone; he and his wife, the stage directions tell us, move in circles of light that represent "auras of egotism" and the high ideals of their marriage are but ways each ego uses to get possession of the other. O'Neill had his answer to this problem of the possessive, discrete personality. Egotism and idealism, he tells us, are twin evils growing from man's suspicion of his life and the remedy is the laughter of Lazarus—"a triumphant, blood-stirring call to that ultimate attainment in which all prepossession with self is lost in an ecstatic affirmation of Life." The ecstatic affirmation of Life, pure and simple, is salvation. In the face of death and pain, man must reply with the answer of Kublai Kaan in *Marco Millions:* "Be proud of life! Know in your heart that the living of life can be noble! Be exalted by life! Be inspired by death! Be humbly proud! Be proudly grateful!"

It may be that the individual life is not noble and that it is full of pain and defeat; it would seem that Eileen Carmody in *The Straw* and Anna Christie are betrayed by life. But no. The "straw" is the knowledge that life is a "hopeless hope"—but still a hope. And nothing matters if you can conceive the whole of life. "Fog, fog, fog all bloody time," is the chord of resolution of *Anna Christie*. "You can't see vhere you vas going, no. Only dat ole davil, sea—she knows." The individual does not know, but life—the sea—knows.

To affirm that life exists and is somehow good—this, then, became O'Neill's quasi-religious poetic function, nor is it difficult to see why the middle class welcomed it. "Brown will still need me," says Dion, "to reassure him he's alive." What to do with life O'Neill cannot say, but there it is. For Ponce de Leon it is the Fountain of Eternity, "the Eternal Becoming which is Beauty." There it is, somehow glorious, somehow meaningless. In the face of despair one remembers that "Always spring comes again bearing life! Always forever again. Spring again! Life again!" To this cycle, even to the personal annihilation in it, the individual must say "Yes." Man inhabits a naturalistic universe and his glory lies in his recognition of its nature and assenting to it; man's soul, no less than the stars and the dust, is part of the Whole and the free man loves the Whole and is willing to be absorbed by it. In short, O'Neill solves the problem of evil by making explicit what men have always found to be the essence of tragedy—the courageous affirmation of life in the face of individual defeat.

But neither a naturalistic view of the universe nor a rapt assent to life constitutes a complete philosophic answer. Naturalism is the noble and realistic attitude that prepares the way for an answer; the tragic affirmation is the emotional crown of a philosophy. Spinoza—with whom O'Neill at this stage of his thought has an obvious affinity—placed between the two an ethic that arranged human values and made the world possible to live in. But O'Neill, faced with a tragic universe, unable to go beyond the febrilely passionate declaration, "Life is," finds the world impossible to live in. The naturalistic universe becomes too heavy a burden for him; its spirituality vanishes; it becomes a universe of cruelly blind matter. "Teach me to be resigned to be an atom," cries Darrell, the frustrated scientist of *Strange Interlude,* and for Nina life is but "a strange dark interlude in the electrical display of God the father"—who is a God deaf, dumb and blind. O'Neill, unable now merely to accept the tragic universe and unable to support it with man's whole strength— his intellect and emotion—prepares to support it with man's weakness: his blind faith.

iii

For the non-Catholic reader O'Neill's explicitly religious solution is likely to be not only insupportable but incomprehensible. Neither St. Francis nor St. Thomas can tell us much about it; it is neither a mystical ecstasy nor the reasoned proof of assumptions. But Pascal can tell us a great deal, for O'Neill's faith, like Pascal's, is a poetic utilitarianism: he needs it and *will* have it. O'Neill rejects naturalism and materialism as Pascal had rejected Descartes and all science. He too is frightened by "the eternal silence of the infinite spaces." Like Pascal, to whom the details of life and the variety and flux of the human mind were repugnant, O'Neill feels that life is empty—having emptied it—and can fill it only by faith in a loving God. The existence of such a God, Pascal knew, cannot be proved save by the heart's need, but this seemed sufficient and he stood ready to stupefy his reason to maintain his faith. O'Neill will do no less. It is perhaps the inevitable way of modern Catholicism in a hostile world.

O'Neill's rejection of materialism involved the familiar pulpit confusion of philosophical materialism with "crass" materialism, that is, with the preference of physical to moral well-being. It is therefore natural that *Dynamo*, the play in which he makes explicit his anti-materialism, should present characters who are mean and little—that, though it contains an Earth Mother, she is not the wise and tragic Cybel but the fat and silly Mrs. Fife, the bovine wife of the atheist dynamo-tender. She, like other characters in the play, allies herself with the Dynamo-God, embodiment both of the materialistic universe and of modern man's sense of his own power. But this new

God can only frustrate the forces of life, however much it at first seems life's ally against the Protestant denials, and those who worship it become contemptible and murderous.

And the contempt for humanity which pervades *Dynamo* continues in *Mourning Becomes Electra*, creating, in a sense, the utter hopelessness of that tragedy. Æschylus had ended his Atreus trilogy on a note of social reconciliation—after the bloody deeds and the awful pursuit of the Furies, society confers its forgiveness, the Furies are tamed to deities of hearth and field: "This day there is a new Order born"; but O'Neill's version has no touch of this resolution. There is no forgiveness in *Mourning Becomes Electra* because, while there is as yet no forgiving God in O'Neill's cosmos, there is no society either, only a vague chorus of contemptible townspeople. "There's no one left to punish me," says Lavinia. "I've got to punish myself."

It is the ultimate of individual arrogance, the final statement of a universe in which society has no part. For O'Neill, since as far back as *The Hairy Ape*, there has been only the individual and the universe. The social organism has meant nothing. His Mannons, unlike the Atreides, are not monarchs with a relation to the humanity about them, a humanity that can forgive because it can condemn. They act their crimes on the stage of the infinite. The mention of human law bringing them punishment is startlingly incongruous and it is inevitable that O'Neill, looking for a law, should turn to a divine law.

Forgiveness comes in *Ah, Wilderness!*, the satyr-play that follows the tragedy, and it is significant that O'Neill should have interrupted the composition of *Days Without End* to write it. With the religious answer of the more serious play firm in his mind, with its establishment of the divine law, O'Neill can, for the first time, render the sense and feel of common life, can actually be humorous. Now the family is no longer destructively possessive as he has always represented it, but creatively sympathetic. The revolt of the young son—his devotion to rebels and hedonists, to Shaw, Ibsen and Swinburne—is but the mark of adolescence and in the warm round of forgiving life he will become wisely acquiescent to a world that is not in the least terrible.

But the idyllic life of *Ah, Wilderness!*, for all its warmth, is essentially ironical, almost cynical. For it is only when all magnitude has been removed from humanity by the religious answer and placed in the Church and its God that life can be seen as simple and good. The pluses and minuses of man must be made to cancel out as nearly as possible, the equation must be solved to equal nearly zero, before peace may be found. The hero of *Days Without End* has lived for years in a torturing struggle with the rationalistic, questioning "half" of himself which has led him away from piety to atheism, thence to socialism, next to unchastity and finally to the oblique attempt to murder his beloved wife. It is not until he makes an act of submissive faith at the foot of the Cross and thus annihilates the doubting mind, the root of all evil, that he can find peace.

But the annihilation of the questioning mind also annihilates the multitudinous world. *Days Without End*, perhaps O'Neill's weakest play, is cold and bleak; life is banished from it by the vision of the Life Eternal. Its religious content is expressed not so much by the hero's priestly uncle, wise, tolerant, humorous in the familiar literary convention of modern Catholicism, as by the hero's wife, a humorless, puritanical woman who lives on the pietistic-romantic love she bears her husband and on her sordid ideal of his absolute chastity. She is the very embodiment of all the warping, bullying idealism that O'Neill had once attacked. Now, however, he gives credence to this plaster saintliness, for it represents for him the spiritual life of absolutes. Now for the first time he is explicit in his rejection of all merely human bulwarks against the pain and confusion of life—finds in the attack upon capitalism almost an attack upon God, scorns socialism and is disgusted with the weakness of those who are disgusted with social individualism. The peace of the absolute can be bought only at the cost of blindness to the actual.

The philosophic position would seem to be a final one: O'Neill has crept into the dark womb of Mother Church and pulled the universe in with him. Perhaps the very violence of the gesture with which he has taken the position of passivity should remind us of his force and of what such force may yet do even in that static and simple dark. Yet it is scarcely a likely place for O'Neill to remember Dion Anthony's warning: "It isn't enough to be [life's] creature. You've got to create her or she requests you to destroy yourself."

THE JAMES BRANCH CABELL PERIOD

Peter Monro Jack

IT WAS BY CHANCE that James Branch Cabell found himself the American master of literary estheticism in the early 1920's and a sort of competitor to the new critical realism and social satire of the day. He had been modestly and consistently writing for fifteen years, read by a few, by Mark Twain and Theodore Roosevelt, heroically praised by Burton Rascoe, and well enough known to the visiting Hugh Walpole, who records that people would say, as if to take away the disgrace of Dreiser and Anderson, "Well, at any rate, there is Cabell." The censorship of *Jurgen* in 1919 finally did what no reader or reviewer was able to do. There is nothing in the book that Cabell had not intimated before—but it is done here to excess, the style more flamboyant, the sexual innuendoes more salacious, the legend more romantic and correspondingly more disillusioned. The censor earmarked it with uncanny precision. It is a corrupt book, as much in style as in substance, alien and insidious, and precisely what the post-war sophisticate was dreaming of. It became the "gonfalon," as one critic put it (they all fell into Cabell's dressy way of writing) of the great enlightenment in style, beauty, freedom and passion, as if none of these had existed before in American literature.

It was freely said then that civilization had come to the American novel with *Jurgen* and, a little later, with *Erik Dorn* and *Peter Whiffle* and *Jennifer Lorn*. The first raptures over these books brought to our shores the very spirit of Rabelais, Voltaire, Balzac, Huysmans, Anatole France, Horace Walpole, Pater, Wilde, Machen, Max Beerbohm and Aldous Huxley ("Crome Yellow" period) and converted a barbarous literature overnight into an airy dome of wit and urbanity, verve, irony and Gallic sophistication. All these names and all these epithets somehow found their way into the reviews and into the inordinate amount of prefaces ordered for each new edition. Mr. Rascoe further wrote that not Ecclesiastes, *The Golden Ass, Gulliver's Travels* or the works of Rabelais had a surer chance of immortality than Mr. Cabell's *Jurgen*. Sinclair Lewis read *Jennifer Lorn* in England and cabled: "At last a civilized American novel," and Carl Van Vechten led a torchlight procession in its honor through the streets of New York. Mencken thought that "an age of oafish faiths, of imbecile enthusiasms . . . of incredible absurdities" somehow redeemed itself because Cabell reminded him of Horace Walpole and Pater. A professor at the Sorbonne lectured: "*At last* an American novelist with a culture and a style of his own, a conscious artist and a man of letters . . . *at last* we are given a holiday from Theodore Dreiser's triviality, Sinclair Lewis's truculence and Anderson's mystic stammering . . . *at last* an American writer who can think freely and who does not ignore *gaie science*. . . . Praise be to the Lord, *Jurgen* was born in 1919, and the rights of the imagination were restored." He then explained Cabell's indebtedness to Anatole France and the others, showing that Cabell's culture and style of his own were in the very best tradition. It may seem a curious way to praise American civilization by pointing out that everything supposedly good in it has been borrowed or stolen.

But the early 1920's were extravagant in judgment as in everything. The end of the War celebrated the "new" freedom, the "new" morality, the new sophistication, the new disillusion. Travel and a wider range of reading had stimulated and corrupted, and broadened and confused, and romanticized and disillusioned the mind in every degree of variance; the only constant was novelty. The alien ethics and esthetics of Mencken and Huneker had prospered almost too well—brilliant young men were dying for them vicariously in novels everywhere from Chicago to Paris, Ulick Invern of Huneker's own *Painted Veils* being the first. The Modern Library had begun its series of cheap reprints with Wilde's exotic and meretricious *Dorian Gray* as No. 1. The new magazines were publishing the cream of the foreign stylists. The *Smart Set* under Willard Huntington Wright (who now writes detective stories under the name of S. S. Van Dine) had James Stephens, Joyce, Beerbohm, Ford Madox Ford and Schnitzler. The *Reviewer* (see Miss Emily Clark's gossipy source-book of the period, *Innocence Abroad*) had Arthur Machen, Ronald Firbank and (of all people) the demonologist Aleister Crowley. The *Dial* and the *Little Review* had the rest. Certainly a new group of artistic masters, if not a new civilization, had arrived. Fabulous vistas of new entertainment, of esthetic possibilities, were opened up to the young writer. It was inevitable that he should attempt the same sensual pleasures, magic of words, intellectual curiosity and romantic irony in his own composition, natural that every imitation masterpiece that seemed to possess these qualities should be extravagantly overpraised.

ii

It is not pretended here that persons and practitioners of fiction as diverse as Cabell, Elinor Wylie, Hergesheimer, Ben Hecht, Van Vechten and Scott Fitzgerald had any common program or general designs on American literature or even common respect for each other. For that matter we have here an older and a younger generation and we cannot imagine Mr. Cabell caring much for Mr. Hecht's life and works. But together they represent in their various ways the surprising impact of estheticism on a postwar American literature, advancing the somewhat belated cause of art for art's sake which had already flourished and died in its several decades in France and England. Briefly it meant a holiday from life, as if living had become intolerable. Escape in some way was the only intelligence. Cabell had his dreams of masterful or sorrowful love in some imaginary Poictesme. Miss Wylie had her dainty *snobisme* with the past, Mr. Hergesheimer had his grossly expensive snobbery with Cuba, Palm Beach and Duncan Phyffe furniture. Mr. Hecht consoled himself with cynical phrases about life, for which he had no good word. Fitzgerald took his college youths on celestial benders, reminding them on occasion, however, to pay the bill. Van Vechten galloped off into literary escapades that suggested and summarized all of his colleagues. How eagerly disillusioned they were of the world! how eagerly optimistic of their own talent! how lovingly praised! and how little they did with their marvelous opportunities.

Without knowing how much it is read, I should say that it is now almost impossible to read the first "civilized American novel" (Sinclair Lewis), "perhaps the only authentic American masterpiece" (Carl Van Vechten)— Miss Wylie's *Jennifer Lorn*. Consider the young reader who opens it for the first time, looks back with bewilderment on everything the novel has done from *The House of the Seven Gables* to *Ethan Frome*, and wonders how anyone could say that this book surpassed all its predecessors. Here is no more than a pastiche of high life in eighteenth-century England, cluttered with bric-a-brac of ye-olde-tea-shoppe variety. It is quite impossible for any of the furnishings, characters, emotions, attitudes or epigrams to behave naturally for one moment. They are not meant to be life, they are art. They are reproduced from museum pieces and they look like museum pieces. When Gerald ate currants he "had upon his Chinese Bristol plate a superb bunch of white currants," when he sat down it was upon an extravagantly rococo armchair with golden scrollwork and Tyrian upholstery, when he dressed it was in his black velvet suit with very rich waistcoat and ruffles of the finest needlepoint Alençon, when he spoke it was to cry " 'Ignore this mummery' in a voice like cracking glaciers." It is said that this is the style and decorum of the

eighteenth century, but even this is falsely said. It is
Regency period, the gilded elegance of the Bulwer-Lytton
novels, once known as silver-fork fiction.

An elegant diversion in literature is nothing to regret,
though we may think its readers are curiously and easily
diverted; but an authentic American masterpiece is not
likely to be made out of this fancy piece of Beaux-Arts
masquerade. Miss Wylie wrote four novels, all acclaimed
in the same fashion. One of them was turned into an
unplayable play, since it was as brittle as the glass its hero
was made of, and another was turned into a Book-of-the-
Month success, since it brought Shelley to America (Miss
Wylie took over Shelley as Miss Lowell took over Keats).
The last, *Mr. Hodge and Mr. Hazard*, was almost good
and simple, like her poems; but her habits of imitation
and affectation were ingrained. She had hoped to write a
"brief symbolic romance of the mind," but her symbol
was still an esthetic snobbism, her mind a literary man-
nerism.

iii

Mr. Cabell has carried this novel of escape, pre-
tense and sophisticated grandeur to the point of exhaus-
tion, to the point at which it becomes a composed
philosophy of life. It is a simple philosophy, to the effect
that life is tedious, disillusioning and scarcely worth the
effort, though it may be somewhat relieved by a dream-
escape. Other writers have made the same observation,
but surely none has had practically nothing else to say and
has reiterated it so monstrously and monotonously. I am
aware that he has expanded this simple belief into a nightmare of egotism and that connoisseurs can discover a
special revelation or concealment in each editing, re-
titling, reprise or auctorial essay in the Storiesende Edition of his complete works. The façade is extraordinarily
impressive and every device of authorship has made it
attractive—probably no author has appeared to such advantage before his public. But nothing can finally dis-
guise the fact that his dreams are less than half as lively

as life and less than half grown-up. They spend an inordinate space explaining or justifying themselves (can it be that Mr. Cabell is not sure of them?) and they spend quite a time merely waiting around to be dressed and written up. And then in the end we find them easily and fatally slipping into vague reveries of sex, languidly chasing or eluding a coy or wanton femininity.

Energy and originality they do not have, logic they need not have; but surely there is some coherence to this immense game of make-believe of the Biography of the Life of Manuel? Since environmental reality is dismissed and character cannot exist without it, we are left with nothing to talk of but the pleasurable esthetic qualities of style and composition. Mr. Cabell has made a curious mode out of a dozen archaic styles from the Bible to Irish poetic drama, by way of Malory and Hewlett, adding to them a hesitating, niggling and uncertain taste in words, as this, from an important speech in *Jurgen*, may testify: "Henceforward you must fret away much sunlight by interminably shunning discomfort and by indulging tepid preferences. For I, and none but I, can waken that desire that uses all of a man, and so wastes nothing, even though it leave that favored man forever after like wan ashes in the sunlight." A sermon on style could be written on these words, and it would be a serious warning to dilettantes. The composition has the same imperfections, ordinarily regarded by devotees as originality. *The Cream of the Jest*, his summary of the romantic quest, is probably the most tortured theme in literary history, the last word in willful obfuscation. The misinterpretation of the top of a cold-cream jar starts Kennaston off on his dream-adventure, as anything very well might; but is it not rather silly to reproduce the top of this cold-cream jar as a prefatory sigil, upside down and carrying the signature of James Branch Cabell in fancy script, spoiling the whole game at the beginning? And is not the game of Jurgen spoiled at the end with the coarse jest of reducing the middle-aged erotic dreamer to a pimp for his ideal love? Mr. Cabell freely admits that writing is merely a game of style and composition. But he plays it himself irresponsibly, beyond rules as well as beyond life, in a region of quite arbitrary personal preferences and romantic choices. While showing every inclination and outward sign of belonging to the small and distinguished company of stylists, he has not, by one notable sentence or idea, made a candid contribution of his own. The masters with whom he has been compared, from Petronius to Rabelais and Voltaire, made their mark out of the life and usage of their times, not out of cloud-cuckooland.

iv

This pure literary estheticism came near to purifying itself out of existence. Ignoring the immediate experience of life and subsisting entirely on literature and the imagination, it could not even succeed in producing good literature. Its influence on the decade was probably good as a stimulant to curiosity, disastrous as a steady diet. The heroes of the younger novelists were all reading Cabell and the French decadents and attempting to bring the exotic glamour of Poictesme to the brothel, week-end hotel, night or country club, Harlem dive, Greenwich Village speakeasy or Chicago house of ill fame. What the gentle and remote Cabell dreamed of as an engaging impossibility they took into the actuality of their lives. Mr. Cabell accepted no responsibility for the vagaries of his characters and clearly recognized that they had nothing to do with the business of living. The others were more direct and daring and plunged into a historic confusion of esthetic theory and practical experience.

Hecht's Erik Dorn tried the experiment of living in and beyond life, experiencing and at the same time refusing all possible value and meaning to experience. When the radical Tesla bursts into the book to say that art should be something beyond mere decoration or dreams for men sick of life, Dorn is unmoved. Completely disillusioned, completely skeptical, dreams to him are as idle as life; nothing is of any avail. "An amusing writer," thought

Tesla, "sometimes violent, and always empty." It was Mr. Hecht's epitaph on himself and the aspect of his age that he melodramatized: esthetically amusing, for a time at least; emotionally violent in its desires and repulsions; morally and socially null.

Its fictional biographer is Carl Van Vechten, the notable playboy and connoisseur of the period, who wrote its fashionable story year by year in novels from *Peter Whiffle* (1922) to *Parties* (1930). His career covers all the styles and esthetic dalliance of his day in its craziest and toniest manners, which it was Mr. Van Vechten's merit to have combined. He is the last and in a sense the most intelligent infirmity of Mr. Cabell's dreams and Miss Wylie's décor. His part was to see them in practice. He pursued their mannerisms and eccentricities, their stylistic sophistications, their incipient erotic violence and perversion, corruption and insidious paresis, into every particular haunt of sin and gin in the prohibition era and in a way that would have horrified the original American sponsors of *think what thou wilt*, which must inevitably lead to *do what thou wilt*; and he did all of it with an agile pen. The story ends with his last novel, a bitter and blighting envoi to the decade of elegant decadence, complete with definitive bibliography and an epigraph from Radiguet to intimate that this was no provincial tragedy. Mr. Van Vechten gave up his parties, said good-by to all that and took to the lucid and amoral art of photography.

Miss Wylie is dead, Mr. Cabell has shortened his name and aim, Mr. Hergesheimer is almost forgotten, and Mr. Hecht is with the movies, where he so admirably belongs. Their esthetic sophistication has narrowed to the value of a nonce-word recorded in the dictionary, and with it has gone a baggage of irresponsible individualism, private follies and foibles, eccentricities and excesses, pretentious characters and imitation styles. They were all too easily and lavishly praised as wonder boys and girls, and the critical and social background gave them no incentive to match their peculiar state of mind against the general state of the world, which may be categorically stated as the only possibility for the development of character. They did not really develop at all, and a great deal of genuine talent was blanketed in a cozy bed of adolescent complacency, with the critics crooning it to sleep.

It seems to me that F. Scott Fitzgerald suffered most from this critical and social irresponsibility. His recent *Tender Is the Night* is a ghost wandering by its former triumphs. But instead of crying Revenge! it is still wondering why it was so foully murdered. Fitzgerald's biography tells half the story: St. Paul, Minnesota; Princeton University (no graduation—1917, the War); first lieutenant, aide-de-camp to Brigadier General J. A. Ryan; advertising-agency copywriter; the *Smart Set*; the novels, 1920–26; the *Saturday Evening Post*. His titles, the best in fiction, tell the rest: *This Side of Paradise, Flappers and Philosopers, The Beautiful and Damned, All the Sad Young Men, Tales of the Jazz Age.* The matter was trivial, mainly a chronicle of how collegians make money and girls, and the style was no better; but there were reservations and an undercurrent of resentment against these silly topics that came to a head in *The Great Gatsby.*

The Great Gatsby is the great legend of the time, since it most clearly understood its romantic make-believe. Gatsby of the magnificent estate in West Egg, Long Island, the fabulous host of the New York smart set with his champagne parties, incredible luxuries and Petronian orgies, his expensive imitation of all the romantic shoddy of the day, is our old friend from the Midwestern autobiographical novels—James Gatz of a small town in Minnesota and a family of shiftless farmers, digging clams for a living until he is picked up by a millionaire and taught the way of the world. He learned, as a matter of fact, the way of the underworld, through his friend Wolfsheim (Arnold Rothstein), and he made his money first (an essential with Fitzgerald, though it is sketchily developed here) and then invented his magnificent legend of superiority and imposed its fantastic conceit for a while on the world. Here for a moment is the dream of the decade come true, an American Night's Entertainment from James Gatz of Minnesota to The Great Gatsby of Long Island, and here also is its first intimation of disaster. The dream ended in death and disenchantment, as it was bound to end. . . . As one reads *Tender Is the Night*, with its charming and evocative writing, one feels how badly Fitzgerald was served by his contemporaries. Had his extraordinary gifts met with an early astringent criticism and a decisive set of values, he might very well have been the Proust of his generation instead of the desperate sort of Punch that he is. But at least he took Cabell's daydreaming into the marketplace, stripped and washed and aired it, and exposed it to the world for what it was, actually; and in this sense he will be remembered as the chronicler of his age, an age that had nothing better to offer than an escape from it by way of Cabell's *Jurgen*.

TWO POETS: JEFFERS AND MILLAY

Hildegarde Flanner

MORE THAN ANY of their contemporaries, Robinson Jeffers and Edna St. Vincent Millay have been known to the wider public that does not read much poetry. Each has expressed a spirit peculiar to the age. Each has rebelled against the standards of puritanical respectability that prevailed when they began writing, but revolt with Mr. Jeffers has never taken the form of health, youth, fulfilment or pleasure that it took with Miss Millay. His attitude is supremely negative, his protest has been set down in tragic and distorted sexual images. Studying history and modern psychology, Mr. Jeffers has reduced human behavior, civilization itself, to a criticism of human motives. The positive individualism of Miss Millay's poetry, bent on seizing and enjoying life in its complexity, was also a criticism of society. But it was limited to the postwar reaction against gentility when the romantic opportunism of Greenwich Village life welcomed young writers and young morals. To the Western poet, choosing remoteness, there fell a task more definite and more susceptible to failure—a long look forward and backward into history to pass judgment on man.

i

Beginning in 1924 with the intricate and incestuous "Tamar," which was followed by "Roan Stallion," the list of Mr. Jeffers's verse narratives includes eight volumes, containing more than a dozen stories and many shorter poems. The unerring psychic unity of a story is one of his capital achievements. In addition he has to an unusual degree mastery of the narrative form and an uncanny ability to impart life. Unless we except the tragic but gentle character of *The Loving Shepherdess,* and to a lesser degree *Dear Judas,* all his themes are of vehemence, intense and frequently frustrated passion, perversion, bitter introspection; and sex being consummated, repeatedly, for the gesture is nearly as common in his dramas as *attitude* and *arabesque* in Russian choreography.

After twelve years of such preference it is of some value to consider whether his choice of spiritual morbidity and self-infatuated decay is as right as it must have seemed to his own feeling all these years. Oddly enough it is still necessary to point out that his painful motifs of introversion are intended as racial symbols of the same evil on a broader and more fatal plane, that of civilization turning in upon itself. His Orestes in *The Tower Beyond Tragedy* clearly achieves freedom from the involvements of humanity. Barclay, in *The Women at Point Sur,* aims and fails of the same mark in testing the socially and biologically abhorrent deed (incest between father and daughter), as a means of liberation from both good and evil. To quote Mr. Jeffers, "Just as Ibsen, in *The Wild Duck,* made a warning against his own idea in the hands of a fool, so *Point Sur* was meant to be a warning; but at the same time a reassertion." Further, the book was intended to be an attempt

> . . . to uncenter the human mind from itself. There is no health for the individual whose attention is taken up with his own mind and processes; equally there is no health for the society that is always introverted on its own members. . . . The book was meant to be a tragedy, that is, an exhibition of essential elements by the burning away through pain and ruin of inertia and the unessential. . . . A valid study in psychology; the study valid, the psychology morbid, sketching the growth of a whole system of emotional delusions from a "private impurity" that was quite hidden from consciousness until insanity brought it to the surface.

Mr. Jeffers has given excellent explanations, needed in part because even the most friendly critics have found him obscure—and this in spite of the fact that at the moment of reading his dramas move with such intensity that it seems of secondary importance to derive a further meaning. He has added to his earlier exegesis in *Solstice*. "The theme of self-contradiction and self-frustration," he says of the introductory piece, "intends to express a characteristic quality of this culture-age." The bothersome question as to the validity of Mr. Jeffers's choice of subjects arises for two reasons, the first of which is the nature and source of his convictions concerning society. Belief in political and cultural good, if he ever possessed it, has been replaced by intense social pessimism and revulsion. He is "quits with the people." His poetry mourns "The hopeless prostration of the earth Under men's hands and their minds."—"Civilization is a transient sickness."—"Humanity is needless." His Cassandra cries, "Cut humanity Out of my being, that is the wound that festers." He is convinced of something very like a mythology of human tension and decay, and to it, as one pointing out the evil, he has promised his best in notable artistry. He has no relation discernible, no mutual cause with movements of his own time beyond the subjective relation, the shared honesty of good art. That, in my opinion, would be sufficient for a mind so independent and so well established both in nature and in creative intelligence.

On the other hand—and this must have been said before—it is evident that the problem of good and evil in his poetry is the result of his radical dissociation from the mass of humanity for whom life goes on urgently without the refined distraction of choice or reflection. Like all mythology, if one may call it that, his contains an important truth. He is striking at the root of a definite social neurosis. Nevertheless, however objective his opinion may seem, it is certainly in great part the result of his own carefully guarded isolation and dislike of "the animals Christ was rumored to have died for." It would be impertinent to offer Mr. Jeffers's work as a proof of mere rationalization. But he has recommended war, the cruelest of man's manias, as a way of cleansing civilization and leading life back to reality. At such a moment one knows that his reasoning about the primitive fundamentals, to which he would return consciousness, has betrayed him.

A second reason for questioning his choice of subject is the nature of tragedy itself. There is a kind of willing insanity in many of his characters that robs them of the essence of real tragedy. They do not resist their own furies. They consume in them. Their fate, with the terrible exception of Cawdor, rarely moves us beyond horror. Mr. Jeffers has kept the true value of his stories symbolic while endowing them with his remarkable realism of style. Crazed with egotistical desire or self-accusation, his people speak with the abrupt and boiling language of gods at the same moment that they are proved to be citizens of California out gathering shellfish. His powers of realism and tempo are miraculous. He has used them now for twelve years on people whose pathology is so absolute that their problems can be only the problems of the mad. What should be tragedy comes alarmingly close to overwrought cataclysm (remember the death scene in *Tamar*), not because our prudery cheats us, but because our sense of cartoon, monstrosity, is nearly provoked. In all his narratives only one character of real importance, Fayne Frazier of *Give Your Heart to the Hawks*, makes any move biologically or spiritually beyond the destruction inherent in the drama. "Annihilation is the most beautiful word" and the one most often made flesh.

The Tower Beyond Tragedy, in contrast, achieves the intention of tragedy and is often a supreme piece of writing. It contains no conflict between the ends of tragedy, of megalomaniac introversion and of realism. Orestes and his salvation do not have to be translated into another set of values to have the desired meaning. He can say, "I have slain my mother. . . . I have cut the meshes and fly like a freed falcon. . . . I have fallen in love outward. . . . I will not waste inward upon humanity." He becomes the tragic act and the emblem of redemption that Mr. Jeffers intends, full of the main ethic he has expounded in his other poems. The story is safe in antiquity, safe in the tragic tradition, doubly safe in the code and system of modern psychologic symbols. But when people of our own earth kill their children, desire corruptly, practise incest, long for annihilation, die slowly in great agony from mercury tablets saved over from another purpose, the formula of tragic introversion becomes, *after repeated use*, worn out. It is in excess of the significance and truth of the puppets it moves. The author, writing on the level of the unconscious, leaves us with faulty reasons for carrying over his symbols into the society for which they should stand as correctives.

To be stressed, and no subject for contention, is Mr. Jeffers's profound relationship with nature. All the elements of earth, water and sky are so fused into his pages that continual weathers blow, fill the world and surge through the drama. Nature is the one state, fierce yet impassive, that this poet respects. Only his isolation on the beaten coast and his experience of the Pacific forests and hills could enable him to bring them, a new country, first to the point of emotion and then to the point of words that so mysteriously preserve their fact. That he has done this for American literature and for the Western earth is, in the record of the civilization he deplores, of some historic moment. He believes that the earth will be comforted only when the cities are "gone down, the people fewer and the hawks more numerous." In the meantime his poetry will, in its strange powers and its beauty of line, continue to be an event in the settling of the American mind on the last shore.

ii

In reading Miss Millay's poetry one is always struck by the thought that she has been fortunate in her time of emergence—or that the time was fortunate in her. After the War and during the early twenties she expressed, particularly for women and for youth, a spirit that was symptomatic of the moment. While this spirit appears in poems that weigh least or too prettily in review, it is significant that it added much to her immediate popularity. She gave voice to a new freedom, a new equality, the right of the woman to be as inconstant in love as the man and as demanding of variety. To what extent it was actually applied as a new ethic by Miss Millay's very numerous admirers one hesitates to say. It was, however, a timely statement of intellectual and biological equality, an aspect of feminism for the first time put into poetry of audacity, lyrical quality and vogue.

It is interesting to note that many of her more serious poems coming at a later period, especially the sonnet sequence *Fatal Interview*, are in celebration of the opposite practice, that of romantic love or what is more crudely (or exactly) called transference. It is this state to which literature is indebted for some of the most treasured examples of the poetic art. It is also precisely this state which is passing, for the moment at least, from contemporary poetry. And not because of advanced feminism, but because of a tendency to explore and hold suspect the sources of such emotion when it appears in spectacular form. There will always be readers who go to Miss Millay, a poet of love, for the vicarious enjoyment of emotion as well as the indelible loveliness of such lines as "Oh, sleep forever in the Latmian cave." Since the sonnets of *Fatal Interview*, however, she has come a noticeable distance from the private drama of the early and middle poems. One cannot prophesy, but it is unlikely that she will return to write of romantic passion and the crises of personal attachment. That something is thus lost from poetry is true. But any gain in objectivity is, after a few years, a gain for feeling and hence for the heart, when it again enjoys authority.

Miss Millay is not to be classed among the "makers" who have left language altered and disturbed by their experiments, and ready for new forms and sensibilities. Such a poet was Father Hopkins. She is one of those who take the known forms that offer the readiest vehicle, technically and emotionally, and thus save themselves much loss of time, much doubt. Of her own day in modernism of intellect, she has yet been nearest another age technically. The sonnet was ideally suited to her wants and she surrendered herself to the iambic line and all the machinery of the form, certain to work and work so musically in her hands. Its good brevity, its psychological moments, its fine style of being a capsule of infinity, the effect of an idea ravished and made quotable, all this she was familiar with. That she was able with no hesitation to accept the continuity of a traditional form meant that she wrote in measures already possessing emotional associations for all readers. There was an exchange of gifts, for the sonnet received something from Miss Millay. She took the principle of surprise common to the final lines and developed it into a clever note of drama. She brought her own New England into the sonnet, the weeds and the weedy ocean. She gave to it, as to her other lyrics, homely and modern details and sometimes the grandeur of folk heroism—like the women of Matinicus, lifted in an unforeseen and local metaphor clean out of time and into pathos. She brought to the sonnet the interest and ferment of conversation. She made the form sophisticated, versatile and highly feminine.

It is not easy now to recapture in one's own words the sense of freshness and transparent revelation that her early lyrics conveyed. In these also it had been her fortune to take frequently a traditional form, the elegy, and make it immediate and tender. Her contribution to method has been chiefly in two directions: an infusion of personal energy and glow into the traditions of lyric poetry, and the deceptively artless ability to set down the naked fact unfortified. She has pleased the fastidious and did not scorn to please the simple. In the controlled excitement of poems like "The Pioneer" and "When Cæsar Fell" and in the sensuous beauty of her sonnets—in these and how many more Miss Millay has given to an always eager public a poetry of indubitable achievement.

It is true, however, that an extravagance of feeling, an

indulgence of legendary anguish that belongs to the ultra places and not to the heart of poetry, have thrived beyond wisdom in her lines. One deplores the overdramatic ring in a brilliant measure. Yet it is equally true that an egotism never weak, and one of the best talents for lyrical anger in all literature, have saved her from a problem that other women poets have been torn by. Miss Millay has never been apologetic about the right to love or to suffer. The state of "Justice in Massachusetts" has been for her a tragic social fact but not one that has left her private facts of experience without validity for her poetry. She has not joined the troubled group of women writers who are unable to believe in the significance of their personal emotions, but whom neither middle-class backgrounds nor life have fitted to be the good proletarian poets they feel they should become.

In *Wine from These Grapes*, Miss Millay made an important progress in attitude. She took a definite step toward saving her mature art from what one now detects in her younger verse as the poet's legend about a poet. She is nearer to the stature of "The solid sprite who stands alone." It is the same power which, in the midst of much beauty and excess, was so apparent in Sonnet XLVI of *Fatal Interview* and is repeated in poems like "From a Train Window" and "The Return":

> Earth does not understand her child,
>   Who from the loud gregarious town
> Returns, depleted and defiled,
>   To the still woods, to fling him down. . . .
>
> Who has no aim but to forget,
>   Be left in peace, be lying thus
> For days, for years, for centuries yet,
>   Unshaven and anonymous;
>
> Who, marked for failure, dulled by grief,
>   Has traded in his wife and friend
> For this warm ledge, this alder leaf:
>   Comfort that does not comprehend.

Miss Millay has carried the mood of the epitaph beyond personal loss. Like Mr. Jeffers, she contemplates the end of civilization. Her mind, however, is on the elegy, not the revulsion. "Epitaph for the Race of Man" is eminent writing. But now that the content of her work is changing, these sonnets still run as smoothly as perfect engines. That is the fate of a traditional measure, no matter how strong may be our sense of continuity in using it. It begins to alarm with the bland ease of the mechanical. One does not ask Miss Millay to forgo the exceptional command of her medium. Yet there could be possible an eloquence neither disinherited nor upstart, an eloquence closer to its own necessity than these sonnets are, a kind of language less dependent on the perfection of the form.

iii

The relation of these two poets to their own day has been simple enough to discern, in terms of rebellion. Their relation to tradition should also be suggested. With Miss Millay it is mainly a matter of technique and an intuitive ease in the emotional style of an earlier and great period in literature. In the case of Mr. Jeffers one feels that his scorn for mankind does in itself largely express his relation to tradition—the tradition of the reformer and the prophet. Mr. Jeffers is a moralist of a harsh but practical order, who feels in his heart that there are too many men and that they clutter up the earth he admires. He offers no encouragement or light to confused humanity, only the warning to man to mistrust man, but he is no less a reformer. There we find his place in tradition, rather than in a comparison to the Greek tragedians. To read "Œdipus," then "Cawdor"—"Medea," then "Solstice" —is to see that the modern poet indicts an entire civilization, or nearly everything that man has accomplished since the beginnings of Christianity. Only time can tell whether the hopes and struggles of this day toward a more decent social order will shame his pessimism. Only time can tell whether the simple forthright rebellion of Edna Millay will seem to the future a more important expression of our century's inquiring mind than Mr. Jeffers's knowledge of the psychological types and his building of a cycle of poetic and vehement dramas upon that modern and controversial word—introversion.

DOS PASSOS: POET AGAINST THE WORLD

Malcolm Cowley

SOMETIMES IN READING Dos Passos you feel that he is two novelists at war with each other. One of them is a late-Romantic, a tender individualist, an esthete traveling about the world in an ivory tower that is mounted on wheels and coupled to the last car of the Orient Express. The other is a hard-minded realist, a collectivist, a radical historian of the class struggle. The two authors have quarreled and collaborated in all his books, but the first had the larger share in *Three Soldiers* and *Manhattan Transfer*. The second, in his more convincing fashion, wrote most of *The 42nd Parallel*, 1919 and *The Big Money*. Although the conflict between them seems to me rather less definite on reflection than it did at a first glance, nevertheless it is real; and it helps to explain several tendencies not only in the work of Dos Passos but in recent American fiction as a whole.

The late-Romantic element in his novels goes back to his years in college. After being graduated from Choate, a good New England preparatory school, Dos Passos entered Harvard in 1912, at the beginning of a period which was later known as that of the Harvard esthetes. The best fictional record of those years has been written by Dos Passos himself, in the section of *1919* that deals with the early life of Richard Ellsworth Savage. But Dos Passos does not discuss the ideas of the period that under-lay its merely picturesque manifestations, its mixture of incense, patchouli and gin, its erudition displayed before barroom mirrors. The esthetes themselves were not philosophers; they did not seek to define their attitude except vaguely, in poems; but I think that most of them would have subscribed to the following propositions:

That the cultivation and expression of his own sensibility are the only justifiable aims for a poet;

That originality is his principal virtue;

That society is hostile, stupid and unmanageable; it is the world of the philistines, from which it is the poet's duty and privilege to remain aloof;

That the poet is always misunderstood by the world, and should, in fact, deliberately make himself misunderstandable, for the greater glory of art;

That he triumphs over the world, at moments, by mystically including it within himself: these are his moments of *ecstasy*, to be provoked by any means in his power—alcohol, drugs, asceticism or debauchery, madness, suicide;

That art, the undying expression of such moments, exists apart from the world; it is the poet's revenge on society.

There are a dozen other propositions that might be added to this unwritten manifesto, but the ideas I have listed were those most generally held. They are sufficient to explain the intellectual atmosphere of the young men who read Pater and Arthur Machen's *The Hill of Dreams*, who argued about St. Thomas in sporting houses, and who wandered through the slums of South Boston with dull eyes for "the long rain slanting on black walls" and eager eyes for the face of an Italian woman who, in the midst of this squalor, suggested the Virgin in Botticelli's "Annunciation." As a matter of fact, it was not Dos Passos who argued about St. Thomas, but he was the one who found the Botticelli Virgin, and it is significant that he found her in the slums. There was more realism even in his early poems than in those of the other young men who contributed to the *Harvard Monthly*; but there was no less yearning after ecstasy and no less hatred of the stupid world that never understands a poet until he is dead.

The attitude I have been describing was not confined to one college and one magazine. It was often expressed in the *Dial,* which for some years was almost a postgraduate edition of the *Harvard Monthly*; it existed in earlier publications like the *Yellow Book* and *La Revue Blanche*; it has a history, in fact, almost as long as that of the upper middle class under capitalism. For the last half-century it has furnished the intellectual background of poems and essays without number. It would seem to preclude, in its adherents, the objectivity that is generally associated with good fiction; yet the esthetes themselves sometimes wrote novels, as did their predecessors all over the world. Such novels are still being published, and are often favorably criticized: "Mr. Zed has written the somber and absorbing story of a talented musician tortured by the petty atmosphere of the society in which he is forced to live. His wife, whom the author portrays with witty malice, prevents him from breaking away. After an unhappy love affair and the failure of his artistic hopes, he commits suicide. . . ."

Such is the plot forever embroidered in the type of fiction that ought to be known as the Art Novel. There are two essential characters, two antagonists, the Poet and the World. The Poet—who may also be a painter, a violinist, an inventor, an architect or a centaur—is generally to be identified with the author of the novel, or at least with the novelist's ideal picture of himself. He tries to assert his individuality in despite of the World, which is stupid, unmanageable and usually victorious. Sometimes the Poet triumphs, but the art novelists seem to realize, as a class, that the sort of hero they describe is likely to be defeated in the sort of society he has to face. Sometimes, but not as a general rule, that society is seen with the accurate eyes of hatred. More often it is blurred in a fog of mere dislike; so little does it exist in its real outlines, so great is the author's solicitude for the Poet, that we are surprised to see him vanquished by such a shadowy opponent. It is as if we were watching motion pictures in the dark house of his mind. There are dream pictures, nightmare pictures; then suddenly the walls crash in and the Poet disappears without ever knowing why; he perishes by his own hand, leaving behind him the memory of his ecstatic moments and the bitter story of his failure, now published as a revenge on the World.

Dos Passos's early books are by no means pure examples of the art novel. The world was always painfully real to him; it was never veiled with mysticism and his characters were rarely symbolic. From the very first he was full of pity for the underdogs and hope for the revolution. Yet consider the real plot of a novel like *Three Soldiers*. A talented young musician, during the War, finds that his sensibilities are being outraged, his aspirations crushed, by society as embodied in the American army. He deserts after the Armistice and begins to write a great orchestral poem. When the military police come to arrest him, the sheets of music flutter one by one into the spring breeze; and we are made to feel that this ecstatic song choked off and dispersed on the wind—like how many others—is the real tragedy of the War. Some years later, in writing *Manhattan Transfer*, Dos Passos seemed to be undertaking a different type of novel, one that tried with no little success to render the color and movement of a whole city. But as the book goes on, it comes to be more and more the story of Jimmy Herf (the Poet) and Ellen Thatcher (the Poet's wife), and the poet is once again frustrated by his wife and the World: after one last drink he leaves a Greenwich Village party and commits an act of symbolic suicide by walking out alone, bareheaded, into the dawn. It is obvious, however, that a new conflict has been superimposed on the older one: the social ideas of the novelist are, in *Manhattan Transfer*, at war with his personal emotions. The ideas are now those of a reformer or even a revolutionist; the emotions are still those of the *Yellow Book* and the *Harvard Monthly*.

Even in *The 42nd Parallel* and *1919* and *The Big Money*, that second conflict persists, but it has become less acute. The social ideas have invented a new form for themselves and have drawn much closer to the personal emotions. Considered together—as they have to be considered—the three novels belong to a new category of American fiction.

ii

In the trilogy ending with *The Big Money,* Dos Passos is trying to write a private history of the thirty years that began with the new century and ended with the crash in 1929. He continues to deal with the lives of individuals, but these are seen in the perspective of historical events. His real hero is society itself—American society as embodied in forty or fifty more or less typical characters who drift along with it, struggle to change its course, or merely to find a secure footing—perhaps they build a raft of wreckage and grow fat on the refuse floating about them; perhaps they go under in some obscure eddy—while always the current sweeps them onward toward new social horizons. In this sense, Dos Passos has written the first American collective novel.

The principal characters are brought forward one at a time; the story of each is told in bare, straightforward prose that describes what they do and see but rarely what they feel. Thus, Fainy McCreary, born in Connecticut, is a printer who joins the Wobblies and later goes to Mexico to fight in the revolution there, but runs a bookstore instead. J. Ward Moorehouse, born in Wilmington, Delaware, begins his business career in a real-estate office. He writes songs, marries and divorces a rich woman, works for a newspaper in Pittsburgh—at the end of fifty-seven pages he is a successful public-relations counselor embarked on a campaign to reconcile capital and labor at the expense of labor. Joe and Janey Williams are the children of a tugboat captain from Washington, D. C.; Janey studies shorthand and gets a job as J. Ward Moorehouse's secretary; Joe plays baseball, enlists in the Navy, deserts after a brawl and becomes a merchant seaman. Eleanor Stoddard is a poor Chicago girl who works at Marshall Field's; she learns how to speak French to her customers and order waiters about "with a crisp little refined moneyed voice." Charley Anderson is a wild Swedish boy from the Red River Valley who drifts about the country from job to job and girl friend to girl friend, till at last he sails for France as the automobile mechanic of an ambulance section.

All these characters are introduced in *The 42nd Parallel* and, except for Fainy McCreary and Charley Anderson, they all reappear in 1919. Now they are joined by others: Richard Ellsworth Savage, a Kent School boy who goes to Harvard and writes poetry; Daughter, a warm-hearted flapper from Dallas, Texas; Ben Compton, a spectacled Jew from Brooklyn who becomes a radical. Gradually their careers draw closer together, till all of them are caught up in the War. "This whole goddam war's a gold brick," says Joe Williams. "No matter how it comes out, fellows like us get the s—y end of the stick, see? Well, what I say is all bets is off . . . every man go to hell in his own way . . . and three strikes is out, see?" Three strikes is out for Joe, when his skull is cracked in a saloon brawl at Saint-Nazaire on Armistice night. Daughter is killed in an airplane accident; she provoked it herself in a fit of hysteria after becoming pregnant and then being jilted by Dick Savage—who for his part survives as the shell of a man, all the best of him having died when he decided to join the army and make a career for himself and let his pacifist sentiments go hang. Benny Compton gets ten years in Atlanta as a conscientious objector. Everybody in the novel suffers from the War and finds his own way of going to hell—everybody except the people without bowels, the empty people like Eleanor Stoddard and J. Ward Moorehouse, who stuff themselves with the right sentiments and make the proper contacts.

In *The Big Money* the principal character is Charley Anderson, the skirt-chasing automobile mechanic, who comes sailing back from France as a bemedaled aviator, hero and ace. He helps to start an airplane manufacturing company (like Eddie Rickenbacker); he marries a banker's daughter, plunges in the stock market, drinks, quarrels with the men under him, loses his grip and gets killed in an automobile accident. Dick Savage, the Harvard esthete of doubtful sex, is now an advertising man, first lieutenant of the famous J. Ward Moorehouse in his campaign to popularize patent medicines as an expression of the American spirit, as self-reliance in medication. Eveline Hutchins, who played a small part in both the earlier novels, is now an unhappy middle-aged nympho-maniac. Don Stevens, the radical newspaper man of 1919, has become a Communist, a member of the Central Ex-ecutive Committee after the dissenters and deviationists have been expelled (and among them poor Ben Comp-ton, released from Atlanta). New people also appear: for example, Margo Dowling, a shanty-Irish girl who gets to be a movie actress by sleeping with the right people. Almost all the characters are now tied together by love or business, politics or pure hatred. And except for Mary French from Colorado, who half-kills herself working as the secretary of one radical relief organization after an-other—except for Mary French and her father and poor honest Joe Askew, Charley Anderson's friend, they have let themselves be caught in the race for easy money and tangible power; they have lost their personal values; they are like empty ships with their seams leaking, ready to go down in the first storm.

The trilogy has been getting better as it goes along, and *The Big Money* is the best of Dos Passos' novels, the sharpest and swiftest, the most unified in mood and story. Nobody has to refer to the earlier books in order to under-stand what is happening in this one. But after turning back to *The 42nd Parallel* and *1919*, one feels a new admiration for Dos Passos as an architect of plots and an interweaver of destinies. One learns much more about his problems and the original methods by which he has tried to solve them.

His central problem, of course, was that of writing a collective novel (defined simply as a novel without an individual hero, a novel of which the real protagonist is a social group). In this case, the social group is almost the largest possible: it is a whole nation during thirty years of its history. But a novelist is not a historian dealing with political tendencies or a sociologist reckoning statistical averages. If he undertakes to depict the national life, he has to do so in terms of individual lives, without slighting either one or the other. This double focus, on the social group and on the individual, explains the technical devices that Dos Passos has used in the course of his trilogy.

There are three of these devices, and it is clear enough that each of them has been invented with the purpose of gaining a definite effect, of supplying a quality absent from the simple narratives that form the body of the book. Take the Newsreels as an example. The principal narratives have dealt, necessarily, with shortsighted people pursuing their personal aims—and therefore the author intersperses them with brief passages consisting chiefly of newspaper headlines and snatches from popular songs. Thus, a chapter dealing with Eveline Hutchins' love affairs in Paris during the peace congress is interrupted by Newsreel XXXIV:

> *How are you goin' to keep 'em down on the farm*
> *After they've seen Paree*

> If Wall Street needed the treaty, which means if the business interests of the country properly desired to know to what extent we are being concerned in affairs which do not concern us, why should it take the trouble to corrupt the tagrag and bobtail which forms Mr. Wilson's following in Paris?

> ALLIES URGE MAGYAR PEOPLE TO UPSET
> BELA KUN REGIME

> 11 WOMEN MISSING IN BLUEBEARD MYSTERY

> Enfin La France Achète les stocks Américains

> *How are you goin' to keep 'em away from Broadway*
> *Jazzin' around*
> *Paintin' the town*

Obviously the purpose here is to suggest the general or collective atmosphere of the given period. A slightly different end is served by a second technical invention, the brief biographies of prominent Americans (which incidentally contain some of the best writing in the trilogy). The principal narratives have dealt with people like Charley Anderson and Dick Savage, fairly typical citizens, figures that might have been chosen from a crowd—and so in order to balance them the author also gives us life sketches of Americans who were representative rather than typical, of men like Woodrow Wilson and J. P. Morgan and Jack Reed who were the leaders or rebels of their age.

The third of Dos Passos's technical devices, the Camera Eye, is something of a puzzle and one that I was a long time in solving to my own satisfaction. Obviously the Camera Eye passages are autobiographical, and obviously they are intended to represent the author's stream of consciousness (a fact that explains the lack of capitalization and punctuation). At first it seemed to me that they were completely out of tone with the hard and behavioristic style of the main narrative. It seemed to me that their softness and vagueness and impressionism belonged to the art novel rather than the collective novel; that they were in contrast and even in conflict with the main narrative. But this must have been exactly the reason why Dos Passos introduced them. The hard, behavioristic treatment of the characters has been tending to oversimplify them, to make it seem that they were being approached from the outside—and so the author tries to counterbalance this weakness (though not with complete success) by inserting passages that are written from the inside, passages full of warmth and color and hesitation and little intimate perceptions.

I have heard Dos Passos violently attacked on the ground that all these devices—Newsreels and biographies and the Camera Eye—were introduced arbitrarily, without relation to the rest of the novel. The attack is partly justified as regards *The 42nd Parallel*, though even in that first novel there is a clearer interrelation than most critics have noted. For instance, the Camera Eye describes the boyhood of a well-to-do lawyer's son and thereby points an artistically desirable contrast with the boyhood of tough little Fainy McCreary. Or again, the biography of Big Bill Haywood is inserted at the moment in the story when Fainy is leaving to help the Wobblies win their strike in Goldfield. Many other examples could be given. But when we come to 1919, connections of this sort are so frequent and obvious that even a careless reader can hardly miss them; and in *The Big Money* all the technical devices are used to enforce the same mood, the same leading ideas.

Just what are these ideas that Dos Passos is trying to present? . . . The question sounds more portentous than it is in reality. If novels could be reduced each to a single thesis, there would be no reason for writing novels: a few convincing short essays would be all we needed. Obviously any novelist is trying to picture life as it was or is or as he would like it to be. But his ideas are important in so far as they help him to organize the picture (not to mention the important question of their effect on the reader).

In Dos Passos's case, the leading idea is the one implicit in his choice of subject and form: it is the idea that life is collective, that individuals are neither heroes nor villains, that their destiny is controlled by the drift of society as a whole. But in what direction does he believe that American society is drifting? That question is more difficult to answer, and the author doesn't give us much direct help. Still, a certain progress or decline can be deduced from the novel as a whole. At the beginning of *The 42nd Parallel* there was a general feeling of hope and restlessness and let's-take-a-chance. A journeyman printer like Fainy McCreary could wander almost anywhere and find a job. A goatish but not unlikable fraud like old Doc Bingham could dream of building a fortune and, what is more, could build it. But at the end of *The Big Money* all this has changed. Competitive capitalism has been transformed into monopoly capitalism; American society has become crystallized and stratified. "Vag"—the nameless young man described in the last three pages of the novel —is waiting at the edge of a concrete highway, his feet aching in broken shoes, his belly tight with hunger. Over his head flies a silver transcontinental plane filled with highly paid executives on their way to the Pacific Coast. The upper class has taken to the air, the lower class to the road; there is no longer any bond between them; they are two nations. And this idea—which is also an emotion of mingled pity, anger and revulsion—is the burden of a collective novel that was the first of its type to be written in this country, and is likely to remain for a long time the best.

iii

But the distinction I have been making in the course of this chapter could easily be carried too far. The truth is that the art novel and the collective novel as conceived by Dos Passos are in opposition but not in fundamental opposition: they are like the two sides of a coin. In the art novel, the emphasis is on the individual, in the collective novel it is on society as a whole; but in both we get the impression that society is stupid and all-powerful and fundamentally evil. Individuals ought to oppose it, but if they do so they are doomed. If, on the other hand, they reconcile themselves with society and try to get ahead in it, then they are damned forever, damned to be empty, shrill, destructive insects like Dick Savage and Eleanor Stoddard and J. Ward Moorehouse.

Long before, in *Manhattan Transfer*, Dos Passos had written a paragraph that states one of his basic perceptions. Ellen Herf, having divorced the Poet, decides to marry a rich politician whom she does not love:

> Through dinner she felt a gradual icy coldness stealing through her like novocaine. She had made up her mind. It seemed as if she had set the photograph of herself in her own place, forever frozen into a single gesture. . . . Ellen felt herself sitting with her ankles crossed, rigid as a porcelain figure under her clothes, everything about her seemed to be growing hard and enameled, the air blue-streaked with cigarette smoke was turning to glass.

She had made up her mind. . . . Sometimes in reading Dos Passos it seems that not the nature of the decision but the mere fact of having reached it is the unforgivable offense. Dick Savage the ambulance driver decides not to be a pacifist, not to escape into neutral Spain, and from that moment he is forever frozen into a single gesture of selfishness and dissipation. Don Stevens the radical newspaper man decides to be a good Communist, to obey party orders, and immediately he is stricken with the same paralysis of the heart. We have come a long way from the strong-willed heroes of the early nineteenth century—the English heroes, sons of Dick Whittington, who admired the world of their day and climbed to the top of it implacably; the French heroes like Julien Sorel and Rastignac and Monte Cristo who despised their world and yet learned how to press its buttons and pull its levers. To Dos Passos the world seems so vicious that any compromise with its standards turns a hero into a villain. The only characters he seems to like instinctively are those who know they are beaten yet still grit their teeth and try to hold on. That is the story of Jimmy Herf in *Manhattan Transfer*; to some extent it is also the story of Mary French and her father and Joe Askew, almost the only admirable characters in *The Big Money*. And the same lesson of dogged, courageous impotence is pointed by the Camera Eye, especially in the admirable passage where the author remembers the execution of Sacco and Vanzetti:

America our nation has been beaten by strangers who have turned our language inside out who have taken the clean words our fathers spoke and made them slimy and foul

their hired men sit on the judge's bench they sit back with their feet on the tables under the dome of the State House they are ignorant of our beliefs they have the dollars the guns the armed forces the powerplants

they have built the electric chair and hired the executioner to throw the switch

all right we are two nations

In another passage Dos Passos describes his visit to a Kentucky sheriff at the time of the Harlan strike:

the law stares across the desk out of angry eyes his face reddens in splotches like a gobbler's neck with the strut

of the power of submachineguns sawedoffshotguns teargas
and vomiting gas the power that can feed you or leave you
to starve

    sits easy at his desk his back is covered he feels strong
behind him he feels the prosecuting attorney the judge
an owner himself the political boss the mine superin-
tendent the board of directors the president of the utility
the manipulator of the holding company

    he lifts his hand toward the telephone

    the deputies crowd in the door

    we have only words against

POWER SUPERPOWER

—And these words that serve as our only weapons against
the machine guns and vomiting gas of the invaders, these
words of the vanquished nation are only that America in
developing from pioneer democracy into monopoly capitalism has followed a road that leads toward sterility and
slavery. Our world is evil, and yet we are powerless to
change or direct it. The sensitive individual should cling
to his own standards, and yet he is certain to go under.
Thus, the final message of Dos Passos's collective novels is
similar to that of his earlier novels dealing with malad-
justed artists. And thus, for all the vigor of 1919 and
The Big Money, they leave us wondering whether the
author hasn't overstated his case. They give us an extraordinarily diversified picture of contemporary life, but they
fail to include at least one side of it—the will to struggle
ahead, the comradeship in struggle, the consciousness of
new men and new forces continually rising. Although we
may seem to Dos Passos a beaten nation, the fight is not
over.

HOMAGE TO HEMINGWAY

John Peale Bishop

ERNEST HEMINGWAY had the chance to become the spokesman of the war generation, or, more particularly, he came
to be regarded as the spokesman of that generation by
those who had not, in their own persons, known the experience of war. The phrase which he had culled from one
of his many conversations with Gertrude Stein and
printed opposite the title page of *The Sun Also Rises*—
"You are all a lost generation"—was destined to *faire
fortune*. And to this he appended another quotation from
the aged and charming cynic of Ecclesiastes, which not
only pointed the title of his book, but linked its own
disillusionment with another so old and remote in time as
to seem a permanent proclamation of the vanity of things.

His own generation admired him, but could also appraise how special his experience had been. It was a still
younger generation, those who were schoolboys at the
time of the War, who were infatuated with him. Hemingway not only supplied them with the adventures they had
missed; he offered them an attitude with which to meet
the disorders of the postwar decade. It was they who accepted the Hemingway legend and by their acceptance
gave it a reality it had not had.

It is as one who dictated the emotions to contemporary
youth that Hemingway has been compared to Lord Byron.
The comparison is in many ways an apt one. The years of
Byron's fame were not unlike the decade after the last
war. The hopes raised by the French Revolution had then

been frustrated and all possibilities of action were being rapidly destroyed by those in power. In the 1920's, the disintegration of the social fabric which began before the War became apparent to almost anyone. Here and there were new faces in politics, but Hemingway, who had worked on a Midwestern paper in his youth, gone abroad shortly after the War as correspondent to a Canadian newspaper, come into contact with the literary diplomats at the Quai d'Orsay, followed the French troops of M. Poincaré into the Ruhr, known Mussolini when he too was a journalist, seen war and government from both sides in the Turkish-Greek conflict, was not likely to rate the new gangsters above the old gangs. It should have been obvious to a disinterested observer in 1922 that there was no longer much prospect of immediate revolution in the countries of western Europe. It was in 1922 that Hemingway seriously began his career as a writer.

He was to become, like Byron, a legend while he was still in his twenties. But when I first met him in the summer of 1922 there could be no possibility of a legend. I had just come abroad and calling on Ezra Pound had asked him about American writers of talent then in Paris. Pound's answer was a taxi, which carried us with decrepit rapidity across the Left Bank, through the steep streets rising toward Mont Sainte-Geneviève, and brought us to the rue Cardinal Lemoine. There we climbed four flights of stairs to find Ernest Hemingway. He had then published nothing except his newspaper work, none of which I have ever seen; so that my impressions could be only personal. From that time until 1930 I saw Hemingway fairly constantly. Since then he has retired to Florida, and I have seen him but once. Any later impressions I have are gathered entirely from his books. I say this to make clear what I shall have to say about the legendary figure.

The legend is, in some ways, astounding. Nothing is more natural than that the imaginative man should at times envy the active one. Stendhal would have liked to be a handsome lieutenant of hussars. But the born writer is, by his very imagination, cut off from the satisfactions of the man of action; he can emulate him only by a process of deliberate stultification. Hemingway, as he then appeared to me, had many of the faults of the artist, some, such as vanity, to an exaggerated degree. But these are faults which from long custom I easily tolerate. And in his case they were compensated for by extraordinary literary virtues. He was instinctively intelligent, disinterested, and not given to talking nonsense. Toward his craft, he was humble, and he had, moreover, the most complete literary integrity it has ever been my lot to encounter. I say the most complete, for while I have known others who were not to be corrupted, none of them was presented with the opportunities for corruption that assailed Hemingway. His was that innate and genial honesty which is the very chastity of talent; he knew that to be preserved it must constantly be protected. He could not be bought. I happened to be with him on the day he turned down an offer from one of Mr. Hearst's editors which, had he accepted it, would have supported him handsomely for years. He was at the time living back of the Montparnasse cemetery, over the studio of a friend, in a room small and bare except for a bed and table, and buying his midday meal for five sous from street vendors of fried potatoes.

The relation of a living writer to his legend may become curiously complicated. If we take the account that Mr. Peter Quennell has recently given us in *Byron: The Years of Fame*, it would seem that superficially the poet at twenty-two had only a very slight resemblance to the picture which the public presently began to compose of him. On the contrary, he seemed to his friends a personable, gay young man, an excellent drinking companion; there was, of course, the limp; and he had, as they may not have known, the consciousness of a bad heredity. Childe Harold was made of emotions only latent in Byron. It was a corollary of his fame that the poet should be identified with Childe Harold in the minds of his admirers. But it was not long before in his own imagination he became Childe Harold. And presently Lord Byron is committing incest with his sister. His conscience required that he complete the fiction by a private action. Byron's public stood as panders beside Augusta's bed.

In attempting to say what has happened to Hemingway, I might suggest that, for one thing, he has become the legendary Hemingway. He appears to have turned into a composite of all those photographs he has been sending out for years: sunburned from snows, on skis; in fishing get-up, burned dark from the hot Caribbean; the handsome, stalwart hunter crouched smiling over the carcass of some dead beast. Such a man could not have written Hemingway's early books; he might have written most of *Green Hills of Africa*. He is proud to have killed the great kudu. It is hard not to wonder whether he has not, hunting, brought down an even greater victim.

Byron's legend is sinister and romantic, Hemingway's manly and low-brow. One thing is certain. That last book is hard-boiled. If that word is to mean anything, it must mean indifference to suffering and, since we are what we are, can but signify a callousness to others' pain. When I say that the young Hemingway was among the tenderest of mortals, I do not speak out of private knowledge, but from the evidence of his writings. He could be, as any artist must in this world, if he is to get his work done, ruthless. He wrote courageously, but out of pity; having been hurt, and badly hurt, he could understand the pain of others. His heart was worn, as was the fashion of the times, up his sleeve and not on it. It was always there and his best tricks were won with it. Now, according to the little preface to *Green Hills of Africa*, he seems to think that having discarded that half-concealed card, he plays more honestly. He does not. For with the heart the innate honesty of the artist is gone, and he loses the game.

ii

The problem of style is always a primary one, for to each generation it is presented anew. It is desirable, certainly, that literature reflect the common speech; it is even more necessary that it set forth a changed sensibility, since that is the only living change from one generation to another. But to an American who, like Hemingway, was learning the craft of prose in the years that followed the War, that problem was present in a somewhat special way. He must achieve a style that could record an American experience, and neither falsify the world without nor betray the world within.

How difficult that might be, he could see from his immediate predecessors; they had not much else to teach. On the one side there was Mr. Hergesheimer, whose style falsified every fact he touched. On the other was Mr. Dreiser, a worthy, lumbering workman who could deliver the facts of American existence, all of them, without selection, as a drayman might deliver trunks. Where, then, to start? To anyone who felt there was an American tradition to be carried on, there was but one writer who was on the right track: Sherwood Anderson. When he was in his stride, there was no doubt about it, he was good. The trouble with Anderson was there was never any telling just how long he could keep up his pace. He had a bad way of stumbling, and when he stumbled he fell flat.

So did Mark Twain, who loomed out of the American past. All authentic American writing, Hemingway has said, stems from one book: *Huckleberry Finn*. How much he was prepared to learn from it may be ascertained by comparing the progress of Huck's raft down the Mississippi with the journey of Jake and his friend from France to Spain in *The Sun Also Rises*. Mark Twain is the one literary ancestor whom Hemingway has openly acknowledged; but what neither he nor Sherwood Anderson, who was Hemingway's first master, could supply was a training in discipline.

It was here that chance served, but it was a chance from which Hemingway carefully profited. There was one school which for discipline surpassed all others: that of Flaubert. It still had many living proponents, but none more passionate than Ezra Pound. In Paris, Hemingway submitted much of his apprentice work in fiction to Pound. It came back to him blue-penciled, most of the adjectives gone. The comments were unsparing. Writing for a newspaper was not at all the same as writing for a poet.

Pound was not the young American's only critical instructor. If Hemingway went often to 70 bis, rue Notre-Dame-des-Champs, he was presently to be found also at 12, rue de Fleurus. There he submitted his writings to the formidable scrutiny of Gertrude Stein. It was of this period that Hemingway said to me later: "Ezra was right half the time, and when he was wrong, he was so wrong you were never in any doubt about it. Gertrude was always right."

Miss Stein, for all her long residence abroad, was American. As she sat in one of the low chairs in the pavilion of the rue de Fleurus, she was as unmistakably American as Mark Hanna; the walls were covered with Picassos; but with her closely clipped masculine head and old-fashioned dress, she might have been an adornment to the McKinley era. And if the problem was to combine Mark Twain and Gustave Flaubert—to convert a common American speech to the uses of the French tradition —it could hardly be doubted that Miss Stein had done it. She had taken up, in her *Three Lives,* where Flaubert left off. In *Un Cœur Simple* he had presented the world through the eyes of a servant girl; but the words through which her vision is conveyed are not her own, but Flaubert's. Miss Stein had rendered her servant girls in an idiom which, if not exactly theirs, is supposed to be appropriate to their mentality. It is, so to speak, a transcript of dumb emotions. Having made it, Miss Stein discovered that she had arrived at a curious formalization of the common speech, which, she presently decided, might be put to other uses than the one for which it was originally intended.

If Gertrude Stein is always interesting in what she sets out to do, the result, once her writing is done, is all too often unsurpassed for boredom. She has told us in her *Autobiography of Alice B. Toklas* that she is a genius. We would have preferred that the statement had been made by someone else, but it happens to be true. Miss Stein has a mature intelligence; her genius, unfortunately, has not yet arrived at the age of three years. Ernest Hemingway, at the time that he came under her influence, was a young man of twenty-three; but he was all of that. Miss Stein had developed a literary medium; but she had no material, at least none that was available to that strangely infantile genius of hers. She had at last realized that proud jest of Villiers de l'Isle-Adam; she had had, quite literally, to let her servants live for her. The relation between a writer and his material is much more mysterious than most critics would like to admit. Miss Stein had led, in Paris and elsewhere, what anyone would call an interesting life. She could never write of it until, leaving the genial baby behind, she assumed the proportions of Miss Alice B. Toklas, her companion, and began writing as an intelligent being of her own years.

Hemingway had an abundance of material. There was a boyhood in the Midwest, with summers in the forests of Michigan, where he had come into contact with the earliest American way of life. There were the love affairs of a young man. There was not one war, but two. He had known in his own person an experience for which Gertrude Stein had vainly sought a substitute in words.

What she taught Hemingway must be in part left to conjecture. Like Pound, she undoubtedly did much for him simply by telling him what he must not do, for a young writer perhaps the most valuable aid he can receive. More positively, it was from her prose that he learned to employ the repetitions of American speech without monotony. (I say this quite aware that Miss Stein's repetitions are monotonous in the extreme.) She also taught him how to adapt its sentence structure, inciting in him a desire to do what Hemingway calls "loosening up the language." She did not teach him dialogue. The Hemingway dialogue is pure invention; he does not talk like his characters, and neither does Miss Stein. And it was not until they had read Hemingway's books that the two ladies of the rue de Fleurus acquired those dramatic tricks of speech.

They are brilliant. But they have deafened Hemingway to the way people talk. In *The Sun Also Rises* each of the characters has his own particular speech, but by the time we reach *Death in the Afternoon* and the extraordinary conversations with the Old Lady, there is no longer even the illusion that there is more than one way of talking. It is a formula, in that book employed with great dexterity and no small power; but it is dramatic only in words; in terms of character it is not dramatic at all.

There is no space here to appraise Hemingway's style with accuracy. It is enough to say that, as no one before him had done, he made Midwestern speech into a prose, living and alert, capable of saying at all times exactly what he wanted it to say. It is no longer the lean unlovely thing it was. Just as Eliot, in such a poem as "Sweeney Among the Nightingales," had shown how by controlling the sound apart from the sense the most prosaic statements could be turned to poetry, Hemingway made this American speech into prose by endowing it with a beauty of accurate motion. It is changed, as a gawky boy may change in a few years to an accomplished athlete; its identity is not destroyed. And here I am reminded of a remark of Hemingway's that it was Napoleon who taught Stendhal how to write. It may be that more than one of the best qualities of this prose was acquired from a careful watching of Spanish bullfighters.

iii

We were in the garden at Mons. Young Buckley came in with his patrol from across the river. The first German I saw climbed up over the garden wall. We waited until he got one leg over and then potted him. He had so much equipment on and looked awfully surprised and fell down in the garden. Then three more came over further down the wall. We shot them. They all came just like that.

It is easy to see how a story like this could convey the impression that Hemingway is indifferent alike to cruelty and suffering. And yet this tale is a precise record of emotion. What we have here is not callousness, but the

Flaubertian discipline carried to a point Flaubert never knew—just as in the late war military control was brought to such perfection that dumb cowed civilians in uniform, who cared nothing for fighting and little for the issues of battle, could be held to positions that the professional soldiers of the nineteenth century would have abandoned without the slightest shame. Flaubert describing an incident, despite his pretending to be aloof, or even absent throughout, is continually intent on keeping his emotions implicit within the scene. The reader is never left in the slightest doubt as to what he is supposed to feel from the fiction. But in this account of the Germans coming over the wall and being shot, one by one, all emotion is kept out, unless it is the completely inadequate surprise of the victims. The men who kill feel nothing. And yet what Hemingway was doing in the summer of 1922, lying on a bed in a room where the old Verlaine had once had lodging, was first remembering that he had been moved, and then trying to find out what had happened to cause the emotion. It is the bare happening that is set down, and only the happening that must arouse in the reader whatever emotion he is capable of according to his nature, pity, horror, disgust.*

But this was a point beyond which Hemingway himself could not go. And in the stories that follow the first little volume published in Paris, he is almost always present in one guise or another. That is not to say, as might be assumed, that these stories are necessarily autobiographical. Wounded in the War, Hemingway was a very apprehensive young man. Indeed, his imagination could hardly be said to exist apart from his apprehension. I should not call this fear. And yet he could hardly hear of something untoward happening to another that he did not instantly, and without thought, attach this event to himself, or to the woman he loved. The narration is still remarkably pure. But there is always someone subject to the action.

For this is another distinction. In Flaubert, people are

---

* Or properly, in the case of this "chapter" from *In Our Time*, self-identification with the doomed German soldiers.—M. C.

always planning things that somehow fail to come off—love affairs, assignations, revolutions, schemes for universal knowledge. But in Hemingway, men and women do not plan; it is to them that things happen. In the telling phrase of Wyndham Lewis, the "I" in Hemingway's stories is "the man that things are done to." Flaubert already represents a deterioration of the romantic will, in which both Stendhal and Byron, with the prodigious example of Napoleon before them, could not but believe. Waterloo might come, but before the last battle there was still time for a vast, however destructive, accomplishment of the will. Flaubert had before him Louis Philippe, whose green umbrella and thrifty bourgeois mind would not save him from flight, and Louis Napoleon, whose plans were always going astray. But even Sedan was a better end than Woodrow Wilson had, with his paralytic chair and his closed room on a side street in Washington. In Hemingway, the will is lost to action. There are actions, no lack of them, but, as when the American lieutenant shoots the sergeant in *A Farewell to Arms,* they have only the significance of chance. Their violence does not make up for their futility. They may be, as this casual murder is, shocking; they are not incredible; but they are quite without meaning. There is no destiny but death.

It is because they have no will and not because they are without intelligence that the men and women in Hemingway are devoid of spiritual being. Their world is one in time with the War and the following confusion, and is a world without traditional values. That loss has been consciously set down.

iv

It is the privilege of literature to propose its own formal solutions for problems which in life have none. In many of the early stories of Hemingway the dramatic choice is between death and a primitive sense of male honor. The nineteen-year-old Italian orderly in "A Simple Inquiry" is given to choose between acceding to his major's corrupt desires and being sent back to his platoon.

Dishonor provides no escape, for in "The Killers" the old heavyweight prizefighter who has taken that course must at last lie in his room, trying to find the courage to go out and take what is coming to him from the two men who are also waiting, in tight black overcoats, wearing gloves that leave no fingerprints. One can make a good end or a bad end, and there are many deaths beside the final one. In "Hills Like White Elephants," love is dead no matter what the lovers decide. "I don't feel anyway," the girl says. "I just know things." And what she knows is her own predicament.

The Spaniards stand apart, and particularly the bull-fighters, not so much because they risk their lives in a spectacular way, with beauty and skill and discipline, but because as members of a race still largely, though unconsciously, savage, they retain the tragic sense of life. In *The Sun Also Rises* the young Romero, courteous, courageous, born knowing all the things that the others— wise-cracking Americans, upper-class British or intellectual Jews—will never learn, is a concentration of contrast. And yet the character in that novel who most nearly represents the author is aware, as soon as he has crossed the border back into France, that it is here he belongs, in the contemporary world. He is comfortable only where all things have a value that can be expressed and paid for in paper money.

The best one can do is to desert the scene, as every man and woman must do sooner or later, to make, while the light is still in the eyes, a separate peace. And is this not just what Hemingway has done? Is there a further point to which he can retire than Key West? There he is still in political America, but on its uttermost island, no longer attached to his native continent.

His vision of life is one of perpetual annihilation. Since the will can do nothing against circumstance, choice is precluded; those things are good which the senses report good; and beyond their brief record there is only the remorseless devaluation of nature, which, like the vast blue flowing of the Gulf Stream beyond Havana, bears away of our great hopes, emotions and ambitions only a few and soon disintegrating trifles. Eternity—horribly to paraphrase Blake—is in love with the garbage of time.

What is there left? Of all man's activities, the work of art lasts longest. And in this morality there is little to be discerned beyond the discipline of the craft. This is what the French call the sense of the *métier,* and their conduct in peace and war has shown that it may be a powerful impulse to the right action; if I am not mistaken, it is the main prop of French society. In "The Undefeated," the old bullfighter, corrupt though he is with age, makes a good and courageous end, and yet it is not so much courage that carries him as a proud professional skill. It is this discipline, which Flaubert acquired from the traditions of his people and which Pound transmitted to the young Hemingway, that now, as he approaches forty, alone sustains him. He has mastered his *métier* as has no American among his contemporaries. That is his pride and his distinction.

THOMAS WOLFE

Hamilton Basso

WHEN Sinclair Lewis, in his Nobel Prize address, paid tribute to Thomas Wolfe's *Look Homeward, Angel,* he spoke of the younger author as "a child of thirty or so, a Gargantuan creature with great gusto of life." Mr. Wolfe is no longer thirty and has published three books since *Look Homeward, Angel,* but most of the critical writing devoted to him still follows the pattern established by Mr. Lewis. Already something of a legend, being the sort of person about whom legends tend to gather, Thomas Wolfe is generally written about not as an author but as a young giant whose feats of drink and gastronomy make those of Paul Bunyan and Mike Fink seem second-class. The fact that he writes books seems to be, at best, only incidental.

It is not my intention to insist upon a separation of the writer from the man. I do not think such a separation desirable or even possible, especially in the case of Mr. Wolfe. So much of his writing stems directly from his personal experience that a certain amount of biographical information must be included in any critical discussion of his books. There is, however, a difference between fact and fancy—and of fancy, in connection with Mr. Wolfe, we have had enough.

Look Homeward, Angel, the book which immediately established Mr. Wolfe as one of the more important American writers, begins in Asheville—a city of some fifty thousand inhabitants situated in that part of western

North Carolina where the southern Appalachians begin to rise into the Great Smokies. It is a region of beauty, one of the most beautiful sections of all America, but Asheville, like certain other American places (New Orleans, for example), has sacrificed much of its natural charm and character to become a tourist center. It has on the surface the air and bustle of a city: shops, hotels, theatres, golf courses, night clubs. Dig beneath the surface, however, as Mr. Wolfe does in *Look Homeward, Angel*, and you unearth something entirely different—a small, parochial, isolated town.

It was here, on October 3, 1900, that Thomas Wolfe was born. His father, William Oliver Wolfe, was a native Pennsylvanian who had learned the craft of stonecutter in Baltimore. Restless, a man of great physical strength and appetites, William Wolfe wandered the country for many years, finally drifting across the mountains to Asheville and setting up his shop there. In his small way he prospered and, in time, married Julia Elizabeth Westall, a member of a hardy, prolific, Presbyterian family native to that section of North Carolina for several generations.

These simple facts already take on an extremely familiar air. Have we not heard them before? Who is William Oliver Wolfe but Oliver Gant? Who is Julia Elizabeth Westall but Mrs. Gant? Who is Eugene Gant but Thomas Wolfe himself? So, at the outset, we come to the frequently asked question: "Is Thomas Wolfe writing his autobiography?" In answer, it is perhaps best to let Mr. Wolfe speak for himself. "My book (*Look Homeward, Angel*) was what is often referred to as an autobiographical novel," he writes in *The Story of a Novel*. "I protested against this in a preface to the book upon the grounds that any serious work of creation is of necessity autobiographical. . . . A man must use the material and experience of his own life if he is to create anything of substantial value."

But this, it may be objected, begs the question by answering yes and no at the same time. That, however, is the only answer that can be made. When Mr. Wolfe says there is not a page in his novels that is true to fact we must take him at his word, and few literary practitioners, I feel sure, will disagree with his statement that our own material is all we have. It is our one single well. When it runs dry, we too run dry. The difference between the autobiographical quality of Mr. Wolfe's novels and that of a novel like Scott Fitzgerald's *Tender Is the Night* or Ernest Hemingway's *The Sun Also Rises* is only one of degree. Just exactly where fact ends and fancy begins, I do not think even Mr. Wolfe can say; but *Look Homeward, Angel* and *Of Time and the River* are, contrary to the belief of many critics, more than mere transcripts of experience. If they compose Tom Wolfe's autobiography it is, as he says in the preface of his first book, the sort of autobiography that Dean Swift wrote in *Gulliver's Travels*. It was this idea that he hoped to convey by the subtitle he gave to *Of Time and the River*—"A Legend of Man's Hunger in His Youth." I think it is fairly safe, therefore, to formulate this general principle: No matter how closely Mr. Wolfe's characters resemble their living prototypes, they have all, in some way or other, been transfigured by the talent and personality of the author. They are, in short, idealistic creations.

This is the point, it seems to me, though not the only point, that most of the critics have missed—notably Henry S. Canby, who, in a recent essay, launched a broad offensive upon the so-called "confessional" school of writers. Dr. Canby seems actually to believe that Wolfe, Hemingway and Fitzgerald—among several others—are simply writing true stories of a somewhat higher order than those appearing in the monthly confession magazines. This, of course, is not true: not any more true than that Dickens was writing "confessionally" in *David Copperfield*, or Tolstoy in *Anna Karenina* (the character of Levin), or even Shakespeare in the soliloquies of *Hamlet*. The difference is again a difference of degree; and the hard, stubborn fact remains that no writer can write of things that lie beyond his own experience and give them any real quality of truth or awareness. The least successful of Zola's novels, it is to be remembered, were those composed principally from his notebooks—and there was never a more painstaking note-taker than he.

ii

Tom Wolfe grew up in Asheville. His childhood was not a very happy time for him. His father and mother were always at war with each other, a conflict of strong and opposite wills that was never fully resolved, and his brothers and sisters had little or no patience with him. Mrs. Wolfe, hitching the family's fortunes to the rapidly rising star of Asheville, opened a boarding-house for vacationists in more moderate circumstances. People came and went, something drab and futile about them all: gossipy, bickering, empty. Tom, before and after school hours, was made to do errands and help around the house. School was as much a torment as his life at home. His schoolmates, like his brothers and sisters, felt he was "queer."

The boy, however, found his avenue of escape: in books, in the world of poetry and ideas. His father had a taste for rhetoric and he passed on this taste to his son. Mr. Wolfe describes him thus: "My father was a man with a great respect and veneration for literature. He had a tremendous memory and he loved poetry . . . Hamlet's soliloquy, Marc Antony's funeral oration, Gray's 'Elegy' and all the rest of it. I heard it all as a child."

This is important not only for the light it sheds upon the earlier passages of *Look Homeward, Angel* but because if, as has been said, Tom Wolfe has returned declamation to American literature (it was Herman Melville who introduced it) his father, it seems apparent, is largely responsible. The hymns to America and to October in *Of Time and the River* (some of the finest writing ever produced by an American) and those to Brooklyn and Fifth Avenue in *From Death to Morning* (of a slightly inferior quality) had their genesis in a boarding-house in Asheville.

These sequences, like much of Wolfe's writing (that two-hundred-page train ride in *Of Time and the River*, for example), are all characterized by a brooding preoccupation with space. "There are going to be some damned fine books written in this country of ours," Wolfe once said to me. "Books with the feeling of the country—its power and magnificence. You can't have a really great novel in this country that lacks the feeling of space."

I often wondered, when I first walked the streets of Tom Wolfe's native place—the range of mountains looming behind the skyscraper city hall whose pink roof looks like a birthday cake left out in the rain—how such a walled-in place produced a writer so deeply conscious, so very disturbed, by the vastness of America. And it was not until I went to live in the mountains of North Carolina and discovered what being hill-bound really means, that I understood that Mr. Wolfe's preoccupation with space—with the bigness of America—is a kind of protest against the isolation in which he was vacuumized as a boy. Those trains that roar across his books are far more than trains; they are symbols of escape—symbols retained from the time when, as a small boy, he delivered newspapers in the back streets of Asheville's Niggertown and heard the wailing of a whistle die upon the night; wondering what lay in the northward direction of the train and determining, some day, to go beyond the mountains and find out.

This moment of adventure, as the reader will remember, is the emotional core of the scene with which *Of Time and the River* begins: young Gant standing on the station platform, surrounded by his friends and relatives, ready to leave for Harvard. Asheville—the life of the boarding-house, the first hesitant sexual adventures, all the young torment—is about to be left behind. These early years are the years covered by *Look Homeward, Angel*. That book, as Mr. Wolfe tells us in *The Story of a Novel*, was begun in 1926—"how, why, or in what manner I have never been exactly able to determine." He was then living in London, unknown, uncertain of himself and his future.

The secret of how, and why, *Look Homeward, Angel*

came to be written is contained, I believe, in the poetic fragment which serves as a kind of preface to the book. It is one of those novels, and how many such novels there have been, written out of loneliness and despair: ". . . *a stone, a leaf, an unfound door . . . which of us has not remained forever prison-pent? Which of us is not forever a stranger and alone? . . . O lost . . .*" It is, despite the "realism" that caused such a furor in Asheville when it appeared, the nostalgic yearning of a provincial (I use the word in its exact meaning) who, in a strange and distant country, longs for the sight of a familiar landscape: familiar faces, familiar voices, familiar feuds. It was born out of a passionate feeling of place, a consciousness of class, of family, of home.

The important accomplishment of Thomas Wolfe is not his "tremendous capacity for living," not his voice, "which sounds as it were from demons, gods and sera-phim," not even his "most successful attempt since Joyce and Proust to instill new blood and life into that withered literary form, the novel." It is much less fancy and literary than that. Thomas Wolfe is unique among our younger American writers in that, using the material of a section, he has managed to surpass mere regionalism and—despite repetition, wordiness and some of the most unsuccessful writing in our literature—to impress that material with the mark of universality.

This statement, I feel sure, will meet with various objections. How about Mr. William Faulkner? Has he not also taken the material of a section and endowed it with universal meaning? I think he has—but a necessary distinction has to be made, involving personal judgments and convictions. The universal quality of a book like, let us say, *The Sound and the Fury* is a quality of mood, of emotion—the same investment of horror that gave Edgar Allan Poe his vogue and influence in France. That of *Look Homeward, Angel* (which I believe is the best book Mr. Wolfe has so far written) is quite different. It rests not upon the evocation of moods (which are universal to begin with) but upon the re-creation of a place and

characters understandable, in the light of their own knowledge and experience, to readers all over the Western
world—witness the book's success in such dissimilar countries as, among others, Soviet Russia and Hitlerite Germany. Am I arguing that Eugene Gant is, of all people,
Everyman? I am not. I am simply saying that, in writing
his legendary biography, Mr. Wolfe has written something
of the autobiographies of us all.

iii

Look Homeward, Angel was published in the fall
of 1929. It was a substantial but not a spectacular success.
A few discerning critics realized its quality, but most of
them, particularly those unhappy professionsals who have
to fill a column every day, either overlooked the book or,
as did Mr. Harry Hansen, reviewed it in the familiar "Ah,
Life, ah, Life" manner. They were not to throw their hats
into the air and dig frantically into the adjective pile, until
1935—when, after six years of incredibly furious writing,
Mr. Wolfe published *Of Time and the River*.

It is difficult to assay this novel properly, even in a space
much longer than this. Sometimes, as in the death of
Gant, it is magnificent. Sometimes, as in certain of the
latter chapters, it is overwritten to the point of exasperation. Let us say, to be brief, that while it gives evidence of
the author's incrcasing ability and power it also testifies to
his apparent unwillingness to submit to the rigid discipline of his craft—that discipline which Tolstoy once
called the most important of all the artist's instruments:
even more important than genius itself. And discipline,
as *War and Peace* illustrates, has nothing to do with
length.

Mr. Wolfe's latest books—*From Death to Morning*, a
book of short stories, and *The Story of a Novel*, which
tells how *Look Homeward, Angel* and *Of Time and the
River* came to be written—must be dismissed with unde-
served briefness. They have neither strengthened nor
weakened his claim to a foremost place among living
American writers. It is still impossible, however, to deter-

mine what his final place in our literature will be. His published work represents—as he himself says in *The Story of a Novel*—only a partial achievement. Were he to stop writing tomorrow, that verdict—which overlooks too much, as all verdicts do—would have to stand.

Mr. Wolfe, however, is not going to stop writing. In *The Story of a Novel* he outlines some of his plans for the future: his program of work, what he hopes to accomplish. He also says, in effect (as he did in certain interviews with the press), that he is going to renounce his former ways and try to do better in the future. That is all very fine, but I much prefer the declaration contained in a letter I had from him: "I have something I'd like you to see but it ain't wrote good yet. You wait—I'll learn 'em!"

Learn 'em I think he will.

POSTSCRIPT:

TWENTY YEARS OF AMERICAN LITERATURE

IN THE PRECEDING CHAPTERS we have discussed some prominent literary figures of the 1920's. We have tried to revalue them as individual writers. But what was their significance as a group? What general tendencies did they represent?

Three of them—Dos Passos, Hemingway and Wolfe— were born after 1895 and began writing in the confused atmosphere of the postwar period. For that reason, they stand somewhat apart from the others, who were born between 1871 and 1892. These older writers began their careers at a time when the genteel tradition seemed most oppressive and disheartening. All twelve of them—even Willa Cather—were directly concerned in the revolt against it. But the preceding chapters seem to show that their revolt took four directions, each of which was embodied in a different group or school.

In the first place, there was a tendency toward socialism —or perhaps I had better say toward American populism or farmer-labor democracy, since few of the writers concerned in it had any great knowledge of scientific socialism as defined by Karl Marx. This school had a longer history than the others; some of its members were already famous during the muckraking and trust-busting days of Theodore Roosevelt's second administration. Upton Sinclair's *The Jungle* (1906) and Jack London's *Martin Eden* (1909) helped to inspire the labor literature of the following decade. At its height around 1916, this tendency was represented by poets like Carl Sandburg, Arturo Giovan-nitti and even Vachel Lindsay; by critics like Van Wyck Brooks, Randolph Bourne and Floyd Dell; by novelists like Ernest Poole and Arthur Bullard; by journalists like Max Eastman, Walter Lippmann, Jack Reed; and by scores of hopeful young writers who gave money to the striking textile workers and revolutionary prose or verse to the *Masses*.

But the strength of this group ultimately depended on the strength of the progressive movement in politics and in labor unionism. After the Treaty of Versailles, and the defeat of the 1919 steel strike, and A. Mitchell Palmer's Department of Justice raids on everybody suspected of being tinged with red—after the country grew tired of fighting for a more democratic government and was eager only for its share of the big money, the socialist movement in literature withered away. Jack London was dead from burning too much daylight; Randolph Bourne was dead of influenza, in the epidemic that had many more American victims than the War; Jack Reed was buried in Moscow beneath the Kremlin wall. Ernest Poole had lost his socialist convictions and most of his talent, simultaneously. Sandburg and Van Wyck Brooks were dispirited; Walter Lippmann had gone more than halfway over to the enemy; and Upton Sinclair, though he had changed not at all—though he continued to write and publish and distribute novel after novel—was now being disregarded except in Russia and Germany. Among the younger writers there were only a few, like Dos Passos and Michael Gold, who kept alive the socialist tradition and eventually formed a bridge to the proletarian novelists of the 1930's.

Meanwhile a second tendency, harder to define, was becoming prominent in the years after 1915. It had first appeared in the group surrounding Mabel Dodge Luhan and her salon. I suppose it could best be described as carnal mysticism, though both these words would have to be explained at length. A letter from a young writer, quoted in Mrs. Luhan's *Movers and Shakers*, states the doctrine in its elementary form. ". . . human flesh and blood, sinew, tegument, bone. That, by the way, is where one finds the mystic in life—not in the saints. The mysticism that has been drenched in the flesh has the color and richness that makes beauty. It is by diving into the flesh that one comes to the limits of the material [world]."

That sounds like a mere echo of Oscar Wilde and the 1890 esthetes. But the tendency I am trying to define was much more complicated; it became mixed with theories like free love and primitivism, equality of the sexes and a simplified form of Freudian psychoanalysis. Finally it developed into the doctrine that all repressions are poisonous and all ideals or conventions false and destructive. The truth lies within: it is a mystical state in which, as Mrs. Luhan wrote, "strangely penetrating intuitions rose to consciousness and I would feel a fire burning in me." But that state is not to be achieved by conscious effort or introspection. Our wisest course is to surrender to natural forces. Instead of striving and racking our minds, instead of making money and being respectable citizens, we should listen to the wise voices of the body—we should let ourselves go, abandon wife and job and family, follow our mood wherever it may lead us, and meanwhile be heartened in our driftings by the laughter of the happy and unrepressed Negroes.

Briefly, that is the plot, or half the plot, of *Dark Laughter*, the most widely read in its time of Sherwood Anderson's novels; the hero runs away with his employer's wife and goes floating down the Mississippi. *Diff'rent*, by Eugene O'Neill, is a drama that argues the spiritually destructive force of a woman's sexual repressions. *All God's Chillun Got Wings* is the tragedy of a Negro in the inhibited white world. *Holiday*, by Waldo Frank, is a novel about a lynching in which all the white people are narrowly puritanical, hateful and envious of the moral freedom that exists among the Negroes. The same tendency appears in many other writers—in Evelyn Scott, for example, and Paul Green and Paul Rosenfeld. In the earlier poems of Edna St. Vincent Millay, it takes the form of a simple revolt against the conventions that kept women from living honestly or recklessly. In Robinson Jeffers it becomes a complicated protest against introspection or introversion, which he compares with incest and portrays in furious sexual symbols. Indeed, so many writers of talent were connected with the movement that it seemed to promise a rich literary development, and this in spite of the faults that it obviously encouraged—masks and mannerisms (as in *The Great God Brown*), baby talk (as in Sherwood Anderson's later novels) and everywhere a quantity of emotional lushness and self-pity. The attitude proved valuable just so long as it was inspiring an author to attack the false standards prevailing in American society. But it was otherwise too passive and subjective: it could not help the same author to reach new standards of his own. Little by little it disappeared from the main current of American writing.

In the years after 1925, a third tendency seemed to be triumphant. Fundamentally it was an attempt to compensate for the pettiness and provincialism of American life by creating a literature that would be cosmopolitan, weary, witty and aristocratic—a literature that would deal for the most part with other times or countries and would approach America only in a spirit of urbane mockery and a carefully mannered style. It was the tendency represented by James Branch Cabell and Joseph Hergesheimer; by Elinor Wylie in her novels; by Carl Van Vechten, Ben Hecht, Lilith Benda, Frances Newman and other writers of what used to be called "the sophisticated school."

They wrote stories or essays that were bejeweled and very often bewildering, but the impulse behind much of their work was simple, homely, even patriotic. They wanted to prove that they were not provincial nobodies, good as bread, but genuine tired citizens of the world. They wanted to prove that even Americans could be as wicked and distinguished as the Continental ironists. And they were cheered along by a school of critics imbued with a mixture of French pedantry, German-beerhall wit and, underneath it, the mid-American booster spirit—critics who compared them to everybody from Petronius and Lucian to Rabelais and Ronald Firbank, and whose mildest term of praise was "authentic masterpiece!"

Many writers of the sophisticated school adopted a pose of indifference that was most clearly expressed by George Jean Nathan in *The Code of a Critic*. "I am," he said, "constitutionally given to enthusiasm about nothing. The great problems of the world—social, political, economic and theological—do not concern me in the slightest. . . . If all the Armenians were to be killed tomorrow and if half the Russians were to starve to death the day after, it would not matter to me in the least. . . . My sole interest lies in writing." Now, there was a great deal of guileless boasting in Mr. Nathan's credo. Anybody who had been following his critical writing in the *Smart Set*, the magazine that represented his group from 1913 to 1923, could see that he was enthusiastic about many things of a social, economic, political or even theological nature. But he tried not to be. He wanted to write, and at the same time to be doggedly indifferent to most of the emotions that are the subject of great writing. He wanted to be a dramatic critic, yet without concerning himself in the slightest with the human conflicts that are the essence of drama. He never even realized that the theatre, which he loved, was being attacked and almost destroyed by economic forces. Eventually he succeeded—with how many others like him—in deadening his sympathies and dehumanizing his reactions to the world. Perhaps the epitaph on all the writers of his school is that they became boring by dint of trying to be bored.

A fourth tendency, one that goes back to the beginning of the period under discussion, and one that still continues, is apparently the exact opposite of the third. Instead of running away from America like the sophisticated writers, a whole group of novelists and poets sat down to describe the American middle class exactly as it was and lived, suppressing not a wrinkle from the faces, not a stupid remark from the conversation, not even a scratch from the parlor furniture. Most of these "critical realists" were connected with some particular district in the Midwest or the South, so that one thought of them almost as congressional representatives—Dreiser of Indiana, Lewis of Minnesota, Masters of Illinois, Stribling of Tennessee, Ruth Suckow of Iowa—and, in their earlier works, Willa Cather of Nebraska, Ellen Glasgow of Virginia, Edwin Arlington Robinson of Tilbury Town, in Maine. Some of them made picturesque discoveries about their various sections, and thereby stimulated a new interest in American life. But in general they had the same disheartening report to make—a report that was summarized by Van Wyck Brooks in his comments on the *Spoon River Anthology*:

> It is quite likely, of course, that Mr. Masters, with a reasonable pessimism, has exaggerated the suicidal and murderous tendencies of the Spoon Riverites. But I know that he conveys an extraordinarily just and logical impression. He pictures a community of some thousands of souls every one of whom lives in a spiritual isolation as absolute as that of any lone farmer on the barren prairie, a community that has been utterly unable to spin any sort of spiritual fabric common to all, which has for so many generations cherished and cultivated its animosity towards all those non-utilitarian elements in the human heart that retard the successful pursuit of the main chance that it has reduced itself to a spiritual desert in which nothing humane is able to take root and grow at all. And yet all the types that shed glory on humankind have existed in that, as in every community! . . . Poets, painters, philosophers, men of science and religion, are all to be found, stunted, starved, thwarted, embittered, prevented from taking even the first step in self-development, in this amazing microcosm of our society.

Reading Edgar Lee Masters's autobiography, you wonder whether some of the aridity and loneliness was not in his own heart. A stunted and thwarted artist himself, except when he wrote his book about Spoon River, he has tended to find stuntedness and thwartedness in every subject he has treated. And the remark can be extended to many other writers in the same tradition. It is true that frustration and cruelty were common, and continue to be common in America, to a degree that nobody would have suspected from reading the novelists popular before 1915. It is true that the critical realists were revolting against a personal situation that was almost intolerable. Yet it was partly lack of color in themselves that impelled them to find drabness everywhere; and it was partly lack of insight and perspective that made the different towns and countrysides described in their novels seem evenly monotonous. They could not see the conflicts or the changes beneath the dull surface of middle-class society.

Fundamentally the impulse that produced their work was not very different from the one that guided Elinor Wylie into the late eighteenth century and James Branch Cabell into the never-never kingdom of Poictesme. Both realists and sophisticates were protesting against the lack of direction and grace and distinction that made American life difficult or impossible for a sensitive artist. And this explains why the two schools, apparently with hostile aims, got along so well together, with Sinclair Lewis beating the drum for Elinor Wylie's novels, with Nathan representing the sophisticates and Mencken the realists in the critical department of the same magazine, and Carl Van Doren buttering both schools with impartial praise.

But the truth is that all four of the tendencies just described were so closely related that individuals might easily shift from one to another. Thus, Floyd Dell became known as a socialist critic, but his first novel was a typical Midwestern autobiography, with elements of sexual mysticism that became stronger in his books during the next three or four years. Sherwood Anderson first appeared as a working-class writer, and in one of his later novels he combined proletarianism with mysticism by describing a textile factory in which the machines were sexual symbols. Cabell has written quite realistic studies of Southern life, and Sinclair Lewis, in his own realistic novels, has passages of fancy prose that suggest an undergraduate Cabell. It is obvious that all these writers were held together by forces much stronger than the attitudes or theories that tended to drive them apart. All of them were fighting simultaneously, in their different fashions, against the same conditions disheartening to creative artists. All of them were middle-class, even those who wrote about factory workers or farmhands, and even the sophisticated novelists who prided themselves on being literary aristocrats; Cabell and Elinor Wylie were about the only exceptions. And all of them, even the socialists, were nationalistic Americans at heart. As Sinclair Lewis said at the end of his Nobel Prize address, they were full of the determination "to give to the America that has mountains and endless prairies, enormous cities and lost far cabins, billions of money and tons of faith, to an America that is as strange as Russia and as complex as China, a literature worthy of her vastness."

ii

There were a few writers prominent during the 1920's who followed none of the tendencies I have just defined. There was, for example, the group loosely known as the Imagist poets—Ezra Pound, John Gould Fletcher, Hilda Doolittle (H.D.) and Conrad Aiken, with Amy Lowell as platform speaker and general publicity agent. They too were in revolt against the genteel tradition, but only in so far as it interfered with the writing of honest and experimental poems. Most of them lived abroad. At first they had little interest in social questions; they were trying to establish literature as an independent country, with a history and geography of its own. Later some of them extended their rebellion into other fields. T. S. Eliot, at first connected with the Imagists, became the most influential poet of the decade. But he had ceased to attack literary or moral conventions; instead he was finding an utter lack of dignity in modern industrial society as a whole. This attitude brought him into curious and partial agreement with some of the academic critics surviving from an earlier era, and notably with the two leading Humanists, Irving Babbitt and Paul Elmer More.

Meanwhile Edith Wharton continued her politely but sometimes passionately disapproving studies of American high life. Robert Frost, untouched by the controversies around him, continued to write poems which beautifully pictured his native New Hampshire, with a Yankee economy of words, but which, as Horace Gregory has pointed out, began by being closer in their essential spirit to the English Georgian poets—Blunden, Thomas, Shanks, Abercrombie—than to any of his American contemporaries.

But the largest of the groups that will not fit into our pattern was the one composed of younger men like Hemingway and Dos Passos who did not begin writing until after the War. Sinclair Lewis talked about them briefly in his Nobel Prize address, throwing some light on their aims and their position:

> There are young Americans today who are doing such passionate and authentic work that it makes me sick to see that I am a little too old to be one of them.
>
> There is Ernest Hemingway, a bitter youth, educated by the most intense experience, disciplined by his own high standards, an authentic artist whose home is in the whole of life; there is Thomas Wolfe, a child of, I believe, thirty or younger, whose one and only novel, 'Look Homeward, Angel,' is worthy to be compared with the best in our literary production, a Gargantuan creature with great gusto of life; there is Thornton Wilder, who in an age of realism dreams the old and lovely dreams of the eternal romantics; there is John Dos Passos, with his hatred of the safe and sane standards of Babbitt and his splendor of revolution; there is Stephen Benét who, to American drabness, has restored the epic poem with his glorious memory of old John Brown; there are Michael Gold, who reveals the new frontier of the Jewish East Side, and William Faulkner, who has freed the South from hoop-skirts; and there are a dozen other young poets and fictioneers, most of them living now in Paris, most of them a little insane in the tradition of James Joyce, who, however insane they may be, have refused to be genteel and traditional and dull.

If he had been speaking about the same group in 1937, Lewis might have omitted one or two of these names and might have added two or three others: Hart Crane, Archibald MacLeish, Edmund Wilson.* But on the whole he showed a gift for choosing the lasting reputations among the postwar writers as among his own contemporaries. It seems rather odd to hear him complaining that he is "a little too old" to join forces with men who belong to the very next decade: Lewis was born in 1885, and even the youngest of the writers he was about to mention—even Thomas Wolfe, that "child of, I believe, thirty or so"—was born by 1900. Lewis had shown no such consciousness of age when speaking of Theodore Dreiser, born in 1871, or Sherwood Anderson, born in 1876. But the War had opened a real gulf between literary generations. The young men who had either served in the army or gone abroad in the early postwar years, and had learned to regard the world as an exciting but meaningless and alien spectacle, felt themselves to be separated not so much by years as by light-years from the writers who had shared the political hopes of Wilson's first administration, before being permanently disillusioned. And this slightly older generation felt, in turn, that the postwar writers were not serious and were "most of them a little insane in the tradition of James Joyce," which is the tradition of the pure artist aloof from political life, from its hopes as well as its disappointments.

But from the standpoint of the genteel tradition, these postwar writers occupied a special position. They refused, as Lewis said, "to be genteel and traditional and dull," but their refusal was not a rebellion. Indeed, they did not feel that rebellion was necessary. Like the writers who preceded them, they hated timidity and joylessness, provincialism and puritanism, but they had ceased to believe that these qualities were specifically American. Having traveled over the postwar world, they had found that people in Dijon and Leipzig and Edinburgh were

* At that time he would *not* have mentioned E. E. Cummings or Scott Fitzgerald, both out of favor in the 1930's.—M. C.

not very different from people in Zenith and Gopher Prairie. They had found, moreover, that the older conventions had lost their power and that young men of the 1920's could do just about what they pleased, so long as they had money to pay for it. They could make love without being thwarted or forced into hypocrisy by puritan restrictions—and one does not have to reread *This Side of Paradise* to learn that many of them did. They could drink without being bothered by public disapproval—and one does not have to reread *The Sun Also Rises* to be reminded that many of them drank a great deal. They could mingle with people of all nations without any sense of inferiority at being Americans—indeed, many of them could be comfortably certain that their own books were as good as the books by men of the same age that were being published in France and England. Yet out of all these advantages, which the prewar writers had fought to achieve, they derived no sense of lasting satisfaction. Having tasted the joys of a free life, having gone on the loose in Greenwich Village, got drunk in Paris cafés and visited the bullfights in Spain, they felt even more despondent than Sinclair Lewis in a prairie town or Theodore Dreiser on the banks of the Wabash—and especially after 1930 they began writing some of the most doleful novels and poems that this country has produced.

There are several good examples. Scott Fitzgerald's first book had been a celebration of wartime youth determined to have its own way, and having it. But in 1934 he finished a long novel, *Tender Is the Night,* in which the principal theme is the complete breakdown of the Americans who have gone to live on the Riviera. Some of them become chronic drunkards, some get killed in speakeasy brawls back in New York, some go crazy—all the best of them are lost, and Fitzgerald wonders "why so many smart men go to pieces nowadays.". . . In 1932 Ernest Hemingway published *Death in the Afternoon,* most of which is an enthusiastic treatise on bullfighting. But the end of it is a prose poem full of regret and tenderness for "the one year everyone drank so much and no one was nasty. There really was such a year," but it has gone now never to return. "Make all that come true again," he cries. But "Pamplona is changed . . . Rafael says things are very changed and he won't go to Pamplona any more. . . . Pamplona is changed, of course, but not so much as we are older." Everything good lies in the past. . . . John Dos Passos is a more impersonal writer, not given to elegies over his own dead youth, but *The Big Money*, published in 1936, is a terrific and, in the end, a lyrical picture of decay and disintegration—almost all the characters, through running after big profits and new sensations, have been transformed into brittle, selfish people continually on the edge of nervous collapse or suicide.

The postwar writers had enjoyed the benefits of the revolt against gentility, and its final limitations are revealed in their careers. They had been liberated from the narrow standards that developed at a certain stage of American middle-class society. But a principal result of this liberation had been to uproot them, to cut them off from the daily hopes and worries of their communities; the loneliness that followed was partly the cause of their laments. In another sense, they were no more liberated than the writers who preceded them. They still saw the world as middle-class people, they still lived on middle-class incomes, they were still as politically powerless as almost all the members of their class. When the panic of 1929 destroyed much of their world, a great many personal philosophies crashed like banking houses. There were suicides among the younger writers; that of Hart Crane was the most conspicuous. Many of his contemporaries— perhaps most of them—revised their opinions and their methods.

To discuss the new writers who have appeared since 1930 is beyond the scope of this book. Indeed, the figures and the tendencies are not yet clear enough for the sort of discussion that has been devoted to Sinclair Lewis and his contemporaries. The two most popular novels of recent years were both of them historical, and I suspect that their popularity was partly due to the glamour in which they invested other ages when issues seemed clearer and standards more firmly fixed. The less popular writers were increasingly preoccupied with social themes; the younger novelists were dealing with textile or waterfront strikes or the struggles of the tenant farmers. It seems to me that no great new writers have as yet emerged. The strength and scope of the new subject matter have not yet been matched by the vitality of the characters or by the imaginative force of the writing. Yet there is promise everywhere and a feeling of discoveries being made.

iii

Looking back on the authors discussed in this book, what shall we say about their period as a whole?

One's first strong impression is of the bustle and hopefulness that filled the early years from 1911 to 1916. Everywhere new writers were appearing and marching forward arm in arm against the old standards of life and culture. Everywhere new institutions were being founded —magazines, clubs, little theatres, art or free-love or single-tax colonies, experimental schools, picture galleries, poetry societies, publishing houses that specialized in the new authors—a whole constellation of groups and movements and communities, some of them businesslike and sane, some affected or crazy, but all of them fathered by the spirit of the age. Everywhere was a sense of secret comradeship and immense potentialities for change. "The fiddles are tuning as it were all over America," old John Butler Yeats the painter used to say, speaking from the head of the big table in Pettipas' restaurant to an audience of struggling poets and critics more tipsy with hope than with Madame Pettipas' red wine. They wanted to prove, all of them, that they were worthy of the exciting age in which they were young.

And yet one's second impression is that this wealth of promises was fulfilled only in part. The fiddles were tuned, and tuned again, but the concert never really got under way. It is true that a great deal of lasting work was produced by the men and women of the new generation.

Novels like *Sister Carrie* and *Jennie Gerhardt*, like *Babbitt* and *A Lost Lady*; books of stories like *Winesburg, Ohio* and *The Triumph of the Egg*; poems like some of those in *Spoon River Anthology*, *Chicago Poems*, *The Man Against the Sky* and *North of Boston*; plays like *Emperor Jones* and *Anna Christie* will be read or performed or imitated for a long time to come; they have made themselves part of the American heritage. During the same years, and based on similar theories, there was an even more impressive production of scholarly or reportorial books that have scarcely been mentioned in our survey— *Ten Days That Shook the World*, *The American Language*, *Main Currents in American Thought*, *Middletown*, *The Flowering of New England*, in addition to the important studies of men like C. A. Beard and Thorstein Veblen and John Dewey.

Yet even in the face of this testimony, one still has the feeling of promises unfulfilled and powers never translated into deeds or works. I do not think that this sense of failure is due to the actual shortcomings of the books we have been discussing. They show lapses in force or dignity that are indeed depressing—not in the case of Dreiser or Upton Sinclair, whose blunders are so enormous that they become almost a virtue and certainly a mark of personality, but rather in the case of Lewis with his continual nasal jokes that end by being more tiresome than the business men they are intended to hit off, and Hergesheimer with his rhythms tortured to hide a simple meaning, and Cabell with his adjectives that ring false, and O'Neill with his bad and tasteless style that can be made effective by good actors, but is as painful to read as freshman themes on Life. The devitalized good taste of Willa Cather's later novels is perhaps still worse than the bad taste of her contemporaries. But worst of all is the realization that hardly any of these writers chose and carried out the work they might have completed. One thinks of all the projects they abandoned—for example the third volume of Dreiser's trilogy that was to be a final comment on *The Financier* and *The Titan* and that for twenty years has been announced in publishers' catalogues without ever appearing; and the labor novel with which Sinclair Lewis was going to round out his picture of American life, the novel for which he interviewed trade-union leaders and made several trips through manufacturing towns and even completed a long scenario, but without ever being able to take hold of the subject. One thinks of Carl Sandburg traveling round the country with his guitar, a great poet hired as an entertainer for businessmen's luncheon clubs; one thinks of Van Wyck Brooks retiring from the field of contemporary letters and writing historical portraits that seem completely insulated from the life that used to inspire him to hope or anger; and one cannot help feeling that the talent of all these writers was somehow being diverted and dispersed at the very moment when their work was being praised most extravagantly.

Something happened to blight the promise that had seemed so rich. In the end one decides that this blight was the War—not the mere effort or the bloodshed, but rather the espionage law, the betrayal of their cause by Socialist leaders, the hopes aroused by Wilson's promises; then after the Armistice the broken pledges, the drive against radicals, the prohibition amendment, and the New Era that represented a complete victory for big business. "America *is* business," Calvin Coolidge said. Before 1917 the new writers had felt, even though they were rebelling, that they were still in the main current of American life— the world was going in their direction, the new standards were winning out, and America in ten or twenty or fifty years at most would be not only a fatherland of the arts but also a socialist commonwealth. Then suddenly all these aspirations seemed ingenuous and the new generation felt itself to be isolated from society; it no longer contained the leaders and comrades of the marching people, but merely the "young intellectuals," buzzing and beating their wings like angry flies—the "intelligentsia," to use the foreign word that marked their strangeness and temporary alienation from the national life.

After 1920 their revolt lost its broader outlines and began to be directed against features of American society that these writers disliked for personal reasons—Mencken, for example, disliked Baptists and yokels; Sinclair Lewis disliked small-town snoopers and small-city boosters; everybody disliked the prohibitionists. By choosing enemies like these, they won dozens of easy triumphs, but the fire had gone out of their fighting. And the writers of the next generation were disillusioned in advance. They did not make the errors in taste of their predecessors—for that they were too well-trained and too careful as workmen—but neither did the postwar writers attempt anything very bold or comprehensive. Only Hart Crane, in his heroic cycle of poems *The Bridge*, and John Dos Passos, in the trilogy ending with *The Big Money*, tried to measure themselves against the great poets or novelists of other ages. Only Thomas Wolfe seemed to write without self-consciousness or the fear of being caught in mistakes.

In the end, the real achievement of the authors discussed in this book seems independent of the works they produced, and partly independent even of the ideas for which they did battle. Somehow they lifted the burden of provincialism that had oppressed and disheartened writers in this country. Somehow they broke the old taboos past mending, and made it possible for Americans to write candidly and unaffectedly about their own lives and their intimate emotions. In opening new subjects to literary treatment they were exactly like photographers inventing a new type of film, one that was sensitive to colors and shadings which the older films had failed to register. But beyond all this, the writers who flourished during the 1920's performed the great task of naturalizing the profession of letters in a country that had come to think of it as a foreign or female accomplishment. They found an audience for serious books and, in spite of their personal failures, they created a new literary tradition, thus breaking a road for the new writers who will come after them.

A LITERARY CALENDAR: 1911–1930

IN OUR LITERARY HISTORY, everything seems to happen in waves and troughs of waves. Exciting years like those from 1912 to 1916, when the "young intellectuals" first came forward in eager ranks, and 1919–20, when they seized power in the literary world almost like the Bolsheviks in Russia, would be followed by other years that seem as dull in retrospect as Death Valley. And the general mood prevailing in any year is a context that helps to explain what a given author was really saying.

Included in this calendar are books that helped to determine the literary climate of their time, or that marked the appearance of important new writers. Also included are literary fashions and a few political events—strikes, trials, anti-Red campaigns—that were reflected in literature. I owe a debt to Frederick Lewis Allen for material taken from *Only Yesterday* and from his article, "Best Sellers: 1900–1935," in the *Saturday Review*. But I got most of the suggestions from autobiographies like those of Lincoln Steffens, Mabel Dodge Luhan and Joseph Freeman, and most of the factual information either from *Who's Who* and *The Columbia Encyclopedia* or else directly from authors and publishers mentioned in the calendar.

Perhaps I should have started with 1910, which was a year marked by deaths in the literary world and by a promise for the future. The deaths were those of Mark Twain, William James, O. Henry and William Vaughn

Moody. The promise was the Harvard class of 1910, which contained such ambitious young writers as T. S. Eliot, Jack Reed, Stuart Chase, Heywood Broun and Walter Lippmann. It is the next year, however, that begins a new era.

1911

The Dreiser year. *Jennie Gerhardt*, his second novel, is published and fought about. The great house of Harper undertakes to reissue *Sister Carrie*, which had been suppressed by its first publisher in 1900, and younger writers will be amazed and inspired by its courage. During the next four years Dreiser will finish three more big novels.

Alfred Stieglitz, the editor of *Camera Work*, is urging writers and painters to be bold in self-expression.

The little-theatre movement is getting under way.

Henry James, who had thought vaguely of living in America after his brother's death, instead goes back to England.

The muckraking magazines, enormously successful until now, are being driven out of business by the withdrawal of advertising. And another blow to them: David Graham Phillips, the most prolific of the muckraking novelists, is shot and killed by a lunatic.

Lincoln Steffens tries to settle the McNamara dynamiting case, but nevertheless the McNamaras go to jail, and Steffens has a lot of explaining to do.

The *Masses* is founded by Piet Vlag.

Best sellers for the year: *The Broad Highway*, by Jeffery Farnol; *The Prodigal Judge*, by Vaughan Kester.

1912

This is "the lyric year"; one hears the phrase everywhere. Books of verse—many of them first books—are published by Robinson Jeffers, Joyce Kilmer, William Ellery Leonard, Vachel Lindsay, Amy Lowell, John G. Neihardt, Ezra Pound, Sara Teasdale and a hundred others.

Poetry: A Magazine of Verse is founded in Chicago by

Harriet Monroe, with Ezra Pound as its foreign editor.

Robert Frost sells his New Hampshire farm and goes to England "to live under thatch."

Edna St. Vincent Millay's first ambitious poem, "Renascence," appears in a poetry anthology also called *The Lyric Year*. Elinor Wylie has poems printed in London.

"The fiddles are tuning as it were all over America," says old John Butler Yeats.

Politically this year is the high point of prewar socialism, with Debs getting nearly a million votes.

The IWW invades the East and wins the Lawrence textile strike, with a poet, Arturo Giovannitti, as one of the two strike leaders.

Best sellers: *The Harvester*, by Gene Stratton-Porter, and *The Street Called Straight*, by Basil King.

1913

The year of Mabel Dodge's salon, in Greenwich Village, and the year when the *Smart Set*, under Willard Huntington Wright, is printing the new Continental writers.

The *Masses* is reorganized, with Max Eastman as chief editor. Jack Reed, also of the editorial board, goes to jail for the Paterson silk strikers (IWW) and stages an impressive strike pageant in Madison Square Garden, but the strike is lost.

Reedy's Mirror in St. Louis publishes many of the new writers, including Edgar Lee Masters.

The Armory Show gives New York its first glimpse of the Cubist and Post-Impressionist painters: "Nude Descending a Staircase."

O Pioneers!, by Willa Cather, her first important novel.

An Economic Interpretation of the Constitution, by Charles A. Beard.

General William Booth Enters Heaven, by Vachel Lindsay.

Sons and Lovers, by D. H. Lawrence.

"Looking back upon it now," says Mabel Dodge twenty years later, "it seems as though everywhere, in that year of

1913, barriers went down and people reached each other who had never been in touch before; there were all sorts of new ways to communicate, as well as new communications."

Best sellers: Winston Churchill's *The Inside of the Cup* and *V. V.'s Eyes,* by Henry Sydnor Harrison.

1914

The invasion of churches by the unemployed (New York City, February and March) and the Ludlow Massacre of striking miners (Colorado, April 20) are widely discussed in magazines—at least till war breaks out in Europe.

Sinclair Lewis publishes his first novel, a weak one: *Our Mr. Wrenn.*

The first issue of the *Little Review* appears in Chicago.

The *New Republic,* edited by Herbert Croly, is "a journal of opinion which seeks to meet the challenge of a new time. . . . The final argument against cannon is ideas."

T. S. Eliot settles in England.

Tender Buttons, Gertrude Stein's experiment in language, is published by a Greenwich Village poet, Donald Evans, and becomes the joke of the year.

Chicago Poems, by Carl Sandburg.

Best sellers: *The Eyes of the World,* by Harold Bell Wright, and *Pollyanna,* by Eleanor H. Porter.

1915

A year of new poets and of quarrels over poetry, with Amy Lowell leading and dramatizing the fight against the conservatives of the American Poetry Society.

Robert Frost comes back to the United States. His *North of Boston* and Edgar Lee Masters' *Spoon River Anthology* are furiously read and debated.

Some Imagist Poets, the anthology edited by Amy Lowell, is furiously debated but not read.

Isadora Duncan comes back from Paris and dances to the "Marseillaise." Frank Harris is back from London with debts and delusions of grandeur. Henry James becomes a British subject.

Of Human Bondage, by Somerset Maugham.

The Harbor, by Ernest Poole, dealing with a strike on the New York waterfront.

Van Wyck Brooks sets the tone of the era in *America's Coming-of-Age.*

Best sellers: *The Turmoil,* by Booth Tarkington, and *A Far Country,* by Winston Churchill.

1916

Greenwich Village is full of European artists escaping the War. Diaghilev's Russian Ballet makes its first American tour.

Mooney and Billings are tried in San Francisco on the charge of having bombed a Preparedness Day parade. Many radicals support Wilson in the presidential campaign because he kept us out of war.

Freud is the new fashion among the intelligentsia: Mabel Dodge gets psychoanalyzed.

The Provincetown Players, now in their second season, produce a one-act play by Eugene O'Neill, *Bound East for Cardiff.*

The New York Society for the Suppression of Vice threatens to bring a criminal suit against the publisher of Dreiser's *The "Genius,"* issued the preceding year. The book is withdrawn from circulation.

James Joyce's *A Portrait of the Artist as a Young Man* appears under the imprint of B. W. Huebsch, one of the new publishers—Alfred A. Knopf is another—who are coming to the support of rebel writers.

The Man against the Sky: Edwin Arlington Robinson is rescued from obscurity.

Life and Gabriella: Ellen Glasgow writes a novel about a Virginia woman in revolt against the genteel tradition.

Sherwood Anderson's first novel, *Windy McPherson's Son.*

Henry James dies on February 28 and Jack London on November 22.

Best sellers: *Seventeen,* by Booth Tarkington, and *When a Man's a Man,* by Harold Bell Wright.

1917

Movements like socialism, syndicalism, pacifism and women's rights, which had been spreading rapidly, are checked by the declaration of war and later by the Espionage Act. Many former Socialists and a few Wobblies become Four Minute Men. Others flee to Mexico or go to jail with Debs.

Charles A. Beard resigns from the Columbia faculty in protest against the dismissal of pacifist professors.

Jack Reed reports the Russian revolution.

The *Masses* is prosecuted and finally suppressed (though it will afterwards reappear as the *Liberator*).

The *Seven Arts,* best of the new literary magazines, dies in October as a result of expressing sentiments painful to its lady angel, who is patriotic.

Dos Passos, Cummings, Bromfield, Hemingway, Sidney Howard, and other writers of the next decade are or soon will be in the ambulance service.

The Modern Library is founded by Albert Boni and Horace Liveright as a cheap reprint series of books appealing to the new generation. Oscar Wilde's *The Picture of Dorian Gray* is its first choice, quite naturally.

Edna St. Vincent Millay and T. S. Eliot publish their first books.

Joseph Hergesheimer succeeds with *The Three Black Pennys.*

Best sellers: *Mr. Britling Sees It Through,* by H. G. Wells; *The Light in the Clearing,* by Irving Bacheller.

1918

The editors of the *Masses* are twice brought to trial under the Espionage Act. Art Young, one of the principal defendants, sleeps through the second trial. Both juries disagree.

New York goes wild on the day of the false armistice.

After being cut dead by his friends and hounded by secret-service agents, Randolph Bourne dies in the influenza epidemic.

Henry Adams dies in March; *The Education* will be published after his death.

Lytton Strachey's *Eminent Victorians* foreshadows a new school of biography.

Best sellers: *The U. P. Trail*, by Zane Grey, and *The Tree of Heaven*, by May Sinclair. First in nonfiction: *Rhymes of a Red Cross Man*, by Robert W. Service.

1919

The year of the great hope and the great disillusionment. In the spring, people are dreaming of an American workers' democracy in a world at peace.

Strikes, most of them disastrous. The Seattle general strike in January, the Boston police strike in September, the coal strike killed by injunction, the great steel strike dying all through the fall.

The Volstead Act is passed in October, over the President's veto.

After Versailles, the Wilson administration goes to pieces and its intellectual supporters retire into apathy or the arts.

The Red scare and the Palmer raids. Sergeant Arthur Guy Empey, the author of *Over the Top*, says, "My motto for the Reds is SOS—ship or shoot." The liberals in the Middle West have to whisper behind locked doors.

It is still permitted to revolt against stupidity and moral snoopers. Mencken brings out his *Prejudices: First Series*. James Branch Cabell's *Jurgen*, after being suppressed and then reissued, is sales-promoted to the rank of masterpiece.

Bonds of Interest, by Jacinto Benavente, is the first production of the Theatre Guild.

Thorstein Veblen is writing for the fortnightly *Dial* and teaching at the New School for Social Research, which has just been founded.

Winesburg, Ohio, by Sherwood Anderson.

Our America, by Waldo Frank.

Ten Days That Shook the World, by John Reed.

The desire to get away from it all, to escape into art or the South Seas: all the middle-highbrows are reading *The Moon and Sixpence*, by Somerset Maugham.

Best sellers: *The Four Horsemen of the Apocalypse*, by Vicente Blasco Ibañez, and *The Arrow of Gold*, by Joseph Conrad, his only appearance on a best-seller list.

1920

The year when the new generation of 1912–15, having abandoned or turned against its socialist hopes, moves forward to the seizure of literary power. *Main Street*, by Sinclair Lewis, is the first genuinely popular novel to embody its moral revolt against the conventions.

Other books of the year that attack the genteel tradition and get favorable reviews are *Moon-Calf*, by Floyd Dell, *The American Credo*, by George Jean Nathan and H. L. Mencken, and *Painted Veils*, by James Gibbons Huneker, the old critic's only novel.

Beyond the Horizon, Eugene O'Neill's first full-length play, is liked on Broadway and gets the Pulitzer Prize.

This Side of Paradise, by F. Scott Fitzgerald, just out of Princeton, reveals the existence of a still younger generation that takes what it wants without bothering to stage a rebellion.

Two rich young men from Harvard, Scofield Thayer and James Sibley Watson, have bought the *Dial*. It dies as a political fortnightly and is reborn in January as an esthetic monthly.

The prohibition amendment takes effect on January 16.

The Palmer raids continue into the spring, after reaching their height in January. All the Socialist assemblymen are expelled from the New York state legislature. But the heresy hunters go too far: even Charles Evans Hughes rebukes them.

William Dean Howells dies in May, having outlived his popularity.

Harding sweeps the country, in the first national election after the passage of the women's suffrage amendment.

Wells's *Outline of History* appears in November. It will have an American sale of more than 1,200,000 copies.

Best-selling novel: *The Man of the Forest,* by Zane Grey. Nonfiction: *Now It Can Be Told,* by Philip Gibbs, and *The Economic Consequences of the Peace,* by John Maynard Keynes, both signs of postwar disillusionment.

1921

Beginning the era of flaming youth, of short skirts and the hip-pocket flask. Beginning also the vogue of the jazz-age novels, most of which are written to titillate the older generation. The flappers themselves read Edna Millay's poetry: *A Few Figs from Thistles,* published the year before, and her new book, *Second April.*

The Aldous Huxley craze starts quietly with *Crome Yellow.*

Erik Dorn, by Ben Hecht, the bad boy of Chicago.

Three Soldiers, Dos Passos's angry complaint against Mr. Wilson's war.

Harold Stearns, author of *America and the Young Intellectual,* shakes the dust of America from his feet. But now all the kids are going abroad "to write one honest novel in an atmosphere free from puritan inhibitions."

Magazines are being founded in Europe for the expatriates: *Gargoyle* in Paris and *Broom* in Rome.

Best-selling novels: *Main Street* and Edith M. Hull's *The Sheik.* Nonfiction: *The Outline of History* and Frederick O'Brien's *White Shadows in the South Seas.*

1922

Much later Willa Cather would say that for her the world "broke in two in 1922 or thereabouts." Why that particular year? It is not a disastrous one; it is not truly eventful, except for its literary importations.

James Joyce's *Ulysses* is published in Paris by Sylvia Beach's American bookshop. Expatriates home for a visit succeed in slipping a few dozen copies past customs officials on the lookout for pornography.

The Proust vogue begins: *Swann's Way* is translated by C. K. Scott Moncrieff.

T. S. Eliot's *The Waste Land* appears in the *Dial*.

Then American books, commencing with *Babbitt*, by Sinclair Lewis, his best novel.

Peter Whiffle, by Carl Van Vechten.

Human Nature and Conduct, by John Dewey.

Civilization in the United States, subtitled "An Inquiry by Thirty Americans," is more like an inquest over the corpse of a man whom everybody disliked.

The postwar generation finds a voice in *The Enormous Room*, by E. E. Cummings.

In Paris it is the Dada year. *Secession* is printed in Vienna at a cost of twenty or thirty dollars an issue. *Broom* moves to Berlin, where the exchange is still more favorable.

Best-selling novels: *If Winter Comes*, by A. S. M. Hutchinson, and again *The Sheik*. Nonfiction: still *The Outline of History*.

1923

A *Lost Lady*, Willa Cather's novel of a world that broke in two.

Jennifer Lorn, by Elinor Wylie—"At last a civilized American novel," Sinclair Lewis cables from England.

"Yes, We Have No Bananas."

Time is founded by Briton Hadden and Henry R. Luce.

Vol. I, No. 1 of the *American Mercury* (dated January, 1924) appears in December with its green cover. Great commotion over Ernest Boyd's article, "Esthete: Model 1924."

Best sellers: fiction, *Black Oxen*, by Gertrude Atherton; nonfiction, Emily Post's *Book of Etiquette*.

1924

The Dada movement can't learn to talk United States: *Broom* dies in Greenwich Village.

In Paris the *Transatlantic Review*, edited by Ford Madox Ford, prints stories by unpublished authors like Hemingway and Kay Boyle.

A. E. Orage comes to New York and spreads the Gurdjieff craze for modified yoga among the tired liberals.

The *Saturday Review*, edited by Henry Seidel Canby, is the first independent weekly since the 1890's devoted (at first) solely to books.

Tamar and Other Poems, by Robinson Jeffers.

Michael Arlen's *The Green Hat* has a horizontal heroine who will reappear in many other novels.

The Seven Lively Arts, by Gilbert Seldes, reveals the ineffable esthetic whatness of Krazy Kat.

Burton Rascoe, friend of the anti-genteel writers, loses his job as editor of the New York *Herald Tribune Books* and is replaced by Stuart Pratt Sherman, the academic Humanist. But Sherman soon goes over to the enemy and begins finding merit in the books that Rascoe had been praising.

Best sellers: *So Big*, by Edna Ferber; *Diet and Health, with a Key to the Calories*, by—if you're curious—Lulu Hunt Peters (women are getting thinner).

1925

This is the high point for the generation of prewar rebels. Their novels of the year include *An American Tragedy*, by Theodore Dreiser, *Dark Laughter*, by Sherwood Anderson, *Arrowsmith*, by Sinclair Lewis, *Barren Ground*, by Ellen Glasgow, and *The Professor's House*, by Willa Cather.

In Our Time, Ernest Hemingway's first collection of short stories, has a sale of less than a thousand copies.

Manhattan Transfer, by John Dos Passos—"More important in every way," Sinclair Lewis says, "than anything by Gertrude Stein or Marcel Proust or even that great white boar, Mr. Joyce's *Ulysses*."

But *The Great Gatsby*, Scott Fitzgerald's best book, has a mixed press.

George Pierce Baker, the teacher of playwrights, moves his 47 Workshop from Harvard to Yale.

The *New Yorker* is founded—"not for the old lady from Dubuque."

Writers are buying farms in Connecticut.

The monkey trial in Dayton, Tennessee.

Best sellers: fiction, *Soundings,* by A. Hamilton Gibbs; nonfiction, *The Man Nobody Knows,* by Bruce Barton.

1926

Another memorable year. Both Hemingway and Faulkner publish their first novels: *The Sun Also Rises* and *Soldier's Pay.* So does Thornton Wilder: *The Cabala.* Hart Crane's first book of poems is *White Buildings.*

The Time of Man, by Elizabeth Madox Roberts.

Gentlemen Prefer Blondes, by Anita Loos.

Nigger Heaven, by Carl Van Vechten: Greenwich Village is moving uptown to Harlem.

In April the Book-of-the-Month Club announces its first choice: *Lolly Willowes,* by Sylvia Townsend Warner.

Sinclair Lewis declines the Pulitzer Prize for *Arrowsmith.*

The *New Masses* takes the place of the *Liberator,* now defunct.

All the highbrows are fighting about, and some are reading, Spengler's *Decline of the West,* which has just been translated.

Best sellers: fiction, *The Private Life of Helen of Troy,* by John Erskine; nonfiction, once more *The Man Nobody Knows.*

1927

The year of circus parades and the big bass drum. The divorce suit of Peaches and Daddy Browning; the murder trial of Ruth Snyder and poor Judd Gray. Five million words are telegraphed from the courtroom during the Hall-Mills trial. Eighteen tons of assorted wastepaper are showered down on Lucky Lindbergh's New York parade.

The Rise of American Civilization, by Charles A. and Mary R. Beard.

In March the Literary Guild announces its first choice: *Anthony Comstock,* a biography and a labor of hate by Heywood Broun and Margaret Leech. A later choice that year is a book-length poem, *Tristram,* by Edwin Arlington Robinson.

Him, by E. E. Cummings, is produced by the Provincetown Players, and produces a scandal.

Mencken's *American Mercury* reaches its peak with a circulation of 77,000.

Transition is founded in Paris; the *Hound and Horn* appears in Cambridge, Mass.

The first *American Caravan,* edited by Alfred Kreymborg, Paul Rosenfeld and Lewis Mumford, collects the new writers into one big volume.

The Magic Mountain, by Thomas Mann, comes out in English.

In May and June the Chinese revolution fails, with the result that the Communist International shifts its world policy. Trotsky is arrested in November.

On the night of August 22–23, Sacco and Vanzetti are executed in Charlestown Prison. The tired liberals who had fought hard to save them relapse once more into discouragement.

Best sellers: Lewis's *Elmer Gantry* and, for nonfiction, *The Story of Philosophy,* by Will Durant.

1928

A dullish year except in Wall Street and Detroit. But perhaps it marks the climax of instalment buying and high-pressure salesmanship—and also of the revolt against them by the highbrows.

The vogue of debunking biographies continues.

Boston, a two-volume novel by Upton Sinclair, deals with the Sacco-Vanzetti case.

Point Counter Point, by Aldous Huxley, is compulsory reading.

Mae West appears in *Diamond Lil.*

"So you sat through all six hours of *Strange Interlude* and thought it was as wonderful as everybody says? And *Lady Chatterley's Lover*—I hear that you bought a copy in Paris. Please will you let me read it?"

In the midst of the boom, most of the general monthly

magazines are losing money. *Everybody's* is the first to go under.

Book publishers are prosperous and are making big advances to their authors, who promptly sail for Europe— like everyone else who has money for the trip. During the year 437,000 Americans leave the country. There is a building boom on the Riviera.

Best sellers: fiction, *The Bridge of San Luis Rey*, by Thornton Wilder; nonfiction, *Disraeli*, by André Maurois.

1929

A year of endings and also, in the literary world, of new beginnings.

Sartoris and *The Sound and the Fury*, by William Faulkner, the first two books in his Yoknapatawpha County cycle.

A *Farewell to Arms*, by Ernest Hemingway.

Look Homeward, Angel, by a new man from North Carolina, Thomas Wolfe.

The Westchester set is reading *Ex-Wife*, of which the moral is that when young wives are unfaithful they shouldn't tell their husbands.

Among the new writers promoted to genius is Evelyn Scott, for her fifth and her only popular novel, *The Wave*.

But the academic Humanists bring out a symposium proving, among other things, that there are no good American writers except maybe Dorothy Canfield.

In *The Modern Temper* Joseph Wood Krutch proves that the moral revolt of his contemporaries leads to disillusionment. In *Middletown* the Lynds and their staff of investigators prove by the best scientific methods that Lewis was right when he wrote *Babbitt*.

The Gastonia strike begins in April. Eventually it will be the subject of at least four proletarian novels and two plays.

There are new casualties among the monthly magazines, including *Munsey's* and *McClure's*. The great *Century*, which had spoken best for the genteel era, becomes a quarterly (in 1930 it will be merged with the *Forum*). The *Dial* ceases publication with the July issue.

Vernon Louis Parrington dies in June before completing the third and last volume of his *Main Currents in American Thought* (the first two had appeared in 1927).

Transition prints the Manifesto of the Word. Harry Crosby signs it.

Men of letters, too, are dabbling in the stock market and getting their fingers burned. On Black Thursday, October 24, the financial crash started with the distress selling of thirteen million shares of stock.

Harry Crosby commits suicide.

Skirts suddenly get longer, bringing back the atmosphere of 1919.

Best sellers: fiction, *All Quiet on the Western Front*, by Erich Maria Remarque; nonfiction, *The Art of Thinking*, by a French abbé, Ernest Dimnet.

1930

A year of skepticism about American business and of curiosity about Russia, especially the Five Year Plan.

The Critique of Humanism shows a reviving interest in social criticism. Michael Gold cracks down on Thornton Wilder.

Jews without Money, by Michael Gold.

The Woman of Andros, by Thornton Wilder.

The Bridge, by Hart Crane.

The 42nd Parallel, by John Dos Passos, is the first volume of a trilogy that will be completed in 1936 with *The Big Money*.

I'll Take My Stand, that is, in Dixie Land: the Southern Agrarians state their case against industrialism.

Apple sellers appear on every street corner. Banks are closing their doors, including the Bank of United States, with fifty-nine branches and four hundred thousand depositors.

Sinclair Lewis gets the Nobel Prize and delivers a famous oration.

Best sellers: fiction, *Cimarron*, by Edna Ferber; nonfiction, *The Story of San Michele*, by Axel Munthe.

A NOTE IN CONCLUSION

Looking back on this record, I get the impression that most of the years from 1921 to 1928 were dull years intellectually, especially when compared with the preceding decade. The scene was dominated by writers who had come forward between 1912 and 1916, the writers in revolt against the old standards. They now had their own publishing houses, and good ones too—Knopf, Liveright, Harcourt, Viking; they had their own magazines like the *American Mercury*, and even their own play-producing groups like the Theatre Guild and the Provincetown Players. But having attained some of their ambitions, and abandoned the rest of them, they had lost much of their fire and combativeness, and certainly they did not write many of the masterpieces that were expected of them. It was not until 1929 and 1930 that literary history once more became eventful.

I have not carried the record beyond those years because it is much harder to choose the significant events of yesterday. But the truth is that most of the tendencies discussed in 1937—proletarian fiction, Marxian criticism, the revulsion against moral laxness, the search for new values—were foreshadowed in the books and deeds of 1929. The only important tendency to be revealed later was the autobiographical tendency announced by Lincoln Steffens' book in 1931. People who had gone through the War and the boom and had watched the growth of a new system in Russia felt that they had lived in three worlds, and hastened to revalue their own past before it was forgotten. Perhaps this calendar and the book as a whole are among the results of that tendency.

M. C.

CONTRIBUTORS TO THIS VOLUME

NEWTON ARVIN, 1900–1963, was graduated from Harvard in 1921 and taught for nearly forty years at Smith College. His books include a *Hawthorne* (1929), a *Whitman* (1938), then in 1950 a *Melville*, which received the National Book Award. The last and best of his works was a *Longfellow* published a few weeks before his death.

HAMILTON BASSO was born in New Orleans, went to college there, and worked on the staffs of three New Orleans newspapers. His first novel appeared in 1929. Since then he has published ten others, of which *The View from Pompey's Head* (1954) has been the most successful. He has also been a staff writer for various magazines, including the *New Republic*, *Time* and the *New Yorker*.

JOHN PEALE BISHOP, 1892–1944, was a Southerner who went to Princeton, where he was a close friend of Edmund Wilson and Scott Fitzgerald. He wrote carefully and, after an early book of poems (*Green Fruit*, 1917), showed no haste to publish. Though primarily a poet, and then a discriminating critic, he also wrote two volumes of fiction, *Many Thousands Gone* (1931) and *Act of Darkness* (1935). His *Collected Poems* and *Collected Essays* both appeared posthumously, in 1948.

ROBERT CANTWELL is the author of two novels widely praised in their time, *Laugh and Lie Down* (1931) and *The Land of Plenty* (1934). Later he published a painstakingly researched biography, *Nathaniel Hawthorne: The American Years* (1948). He has been a staff writer for various magazines, including the *New Republic, Fortune, Time* and *Newsweek*.

JOHN CHAMBERLAIN was the first daily book reviewer for the New York *Times* (1933–36) and helped to win a hearing for proletarian novels. Later he was book editor of *Harper's* (1939–47). Most of his own books, however—like most of his magazine and newspaper writings—have dealt with politics or business from an increasingly conservative point of view.

MALCOLM COWLEY, who edited this volume, was literary editor of the *New Republic* from 1930 to 1940; later he became literary adviser of the Viking Press. His books include *Exile's Return* (1934) and *The Literary Situation* (1954).

HILDEGARDE FLANNER was born in Indianapolis and educated at Sweet Briar College and the University of California. Besides contributing poems and critical articles to magazines, she has published several volumes of verse, including *Time's Profile* and *If There Is Time*.

PETER MONRO JACK, 1896–1944, was born in Scotland and educated at Aberdeen University and at Cambridge, where he studied under I. A. Richards. He came to this country in 1927 to teach at the University of Michigan. In 1930 he moved to New York City, where he became a lecturer and a free-lance writer. His excellent critical articles, printed in a variety of magazines, have never been collected.

LOUIS KRONENBERGER was one of the young men who got their introduction to the literary world by serving as junior editors for Boni and Liveright, then—in 1926—the most exciting of the "new-line" publishers. His first book was a novel, *The Grand Manner* (1929). Since then he has written or edited a diversity of books, including several in the field of eighteenth-century literature. He was theatre critic of *Time* magazine from 1938 to 1962. A year later he was named librarian of Brandeis University.

ROBERT MORSS LOVETT, 1870–1956, was graduated from Harvard in 1892 and then, after a postgraduate year, joined the faculty of the newly established University of Chicago, where he served until 1936. His two close friends there were the novelist Robert Herrick and the poet William Vaughn Moody, with the second of whom he wrote a very successful *History of English Literature*. Always a crusader for civil liberties, he became involved in some famous controversies, of which he gives an even-tempered account in his autobiography, *All Our Years* (1948).

BERNARD SMITH, during the thirties and forties, wrote many articles on American and modern European literature for the *New Republic*, the New York *Times*, the *Saturday Review* and other magazines. Among books that he edited, and for which he wrote introductions, were a big anthology, *The Democratic Spirit*, and *The Complete Poetry of Walt Whitman*.

LIONEL TRILLING, who has taught at Columbia since 1931, was not yet widely known when he wrote the two essays in this volume. His first book, *Matthew Arnold*, was published two years later, in 1939. Since then he has written several distinguished critical works, including *The Liberal Imagination* (1950) and *The Opposing Self* (1955), as well as a novel, *The Middle of the Journey* (1947).